05/01

19.96

The Liberator

Voice of the Abolitionist Movement

**Titles in the
Words That Changed History series include:**

Words
T H A T
CHANGED
HISTORY

The Liberator
Voice of the Abolitionist Movement

by Stephen Currie

Lucent Books
P.O. Box 289011, San Diego, CA 92198-9011

Library of Congress Cataloging-in-Publication Data

Currie, Stephen, 1960–
    The Liberator: voice of the abolitionist movement / by Stephen Currie.
        p.   cm. — (Words that changed history)
    Includes bibliographical references and index.
    Summary: Discusses the abolitionist newspaper, the Liberator, and its
    founder William Garrison, describing its role in the antislavery movement,
    its philosophy, reactions to it, and its legacy.
    ISBN 1-56006-672-5 (lib. bdg. : alk. paper)
        1. Liberator (Boston, Mass.)—Juvenile literature. 2. Antislavery
    movements—United States—Periodicals—History—Juvenile literature.
    3. Slavery—United States—Periodicals—History—Juvenile literature.
    4. Antislavery movements—United States—History—19th century—
    Juvenile literature. 5. Slavery—United States—History—19th century—
    Juvenile literature. 6. Garrison, William Lloyd, 1805–1879—Juvenile
    literature. [1. Liberator (Boston, Mass.). 2. Antislavery movements.
    3. American newspapers. 4. Garrison, William Lloyd, 1805–1879.]
    I. Title.   II. Series.
    E449.C974—2000
    973.7'114 21—dc21   99-041296

Copyright 2000 by Lucent Books, Inc.
P.O. Box 289011, San Diego, California 92198-9011

Printed in the U.S.A.

Contents

Foreword

"We hold these truths to be self-evident, that all men are created equal, that they are endowed by their Creator with certain unalienable Rights, that among these are Life, Liberty and the pursuit of Happiness." So states one of America's most cherished documents, the Declaration of Independence. These words ripple through time. They represent the thoughts of the Declaration's author, Thomas Jefferson, but at the same time they reflect the attitudes of a nation in which individual rights were trampled by a foreign government. To many of Jefferson's contemporaries, these words characterized a revolutionary philosophy of liberty. Many Americans today still believe the ideas expressed in the Declaration were uniquely American. And while it is true that this document was a product of American ideals and values, its ideas did not spring from an intellectual vacuum. The Enlightenment which had pervaded France and England for years had proffered ideas of individual rights, and Enlightenment scholars drew their notions from historical antecedents tracing back to ancient Greece.

In essence, the Declaration was part of an ongoing historical dialogue concerning the conflict between individual rights and government powers. There is no doubt, however, that it made a palpable impact on its times. For colonists, the Declaration listed their grievances and set out the ideas for which they would stand and fight. These words changed history for Americans. But the Declaration also changed history for other nations; in France, revolutionaries would emulate concepts of self-rule to bring down their own monarchy and draft their own philosophies in a document known as the Declaration of the Rights of Man and of the Citizen. And the historical dialogue continues today in many third world nations.

Lucent Books's Words That Changed History series looks at oral and written documents in light of their historical context and their lasting impact. Some documents, such as the Declaration, spurred people to immediately change society; other documents fostered lasting intellectual debate. For example, Charles Darwin's treatise *On the Origin of Species* did not simply extend the discussion of human origins, it offered a theory of evolution which eventually would cause a schism between some religious and scientific thinkers. The debate still rages as people on both sides reaffirm their intellectual positions, even as new scientific evidence continues to impact the issue.

Students researching famous documents, the time periods in which they were prominent, or the issues they raise will find the books in this series both compelling and useful. Readers will see the chain of events that give rise to historical events. They will understand through the examination of specific documents that ideas or philosophies always have their antecedents, and they will learn how these documents carried on the legacy of influence by affecting people in other places or other times. The format for the series emphasizes these points by devoting chapters to the political or intellectual climate of the times, the values and prejudices of the drafters or speakers, the contents of the document and its impact on its contemporaries, and the manner in which perceptions of the document have changed through time.

In addition to their format, the books in Lucent's Words That Changed History series contain features that enhance understanding. Many primary and secondary source quotes give readers insight into the thoughts of the document's contemporaries as well as those who interpret the document's significance in hindsight. Sidebars interspersed throughout the text offer greater examination of relevant personages or significant events to provide readers with a broader historical context. Footnotes allow readers to verify the credibility of source material. Two bibliographies give students the opportunity to expand their research. And an appendix that includes excerpts as well as full text of original documents gives students access to the larger historical picture into which these documents fit.

History is often shaped by words. Oral and written documents concretize the thoughts of a select few, but they often transform the beliefs of an entire era or nation. As Confucius asserted, "Without knowing the force of words, it is impossible to know men." And understanding the power of words reveals a new way of understanding history.

Introduction

The *Liberator* in Its Time

Compared with other American newspapers of the early 1830s, William Lloyd Garrison's *Liberator* seemed to have little to recommend it. A four-page Boston-based weekly with low circulation, the *Liberator* could not match in size or readership the larger big-city newspapers of its time. Other newspapers had reporting staffs; Garrison wrote nearly every word of the *Liberator* himself, often working only with the help of one assistant printer. And while competing newspapers covered a wide range of local and national issues, Garrison's paper stuck mainly to a single theme and a single purpose: the immediate abolition of slavery, a goal not shared by many other Americans of the period. On the surface, at least, the *Liberator* ought to occupy a minor place in American history.

Yet the *Liberator* was not at all the obscure circular one might have expected. During its more than thirty years of publication, from 1831 to 1865, the little paper had an influence far outweighing its small size and limited distribution. Garrison's uncompromising zeal for immediate abolition soon won his paper national notice. His stubborn quest for justice and equal rights for all—including blacks and women—led him to sound the same message again and again, always in strident and intense tones. The newspaper did not avoid controversy: on the contrary, the *Liberator* stirred up trouble wherever it could.

Reactions to Garrison's message varied considerably. Free blacks and a few other white abolitionists saw Garrison as a leading proponent of their cause and wholeheartedly supported the *Liberator*. On

Front page heading of the Liberator *newspaper, which called for the abolition of slavery.*

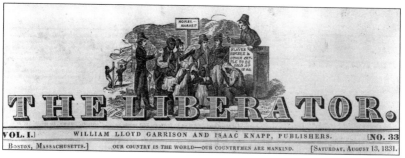

the other hand, many abolitionists less radical than Garrison disliked the newspaper's continued emphasis on immediate emancipation for all. The more pragmatic saw Garrison's goals as unreachable and overly idealistic, and preferred to work toward more gradual emancipation plans that they thought would be more palatable to Southern slaveholders. Garrison did not seek the support of these abolitionists. Instead, he insulted them regularly in the pages of the *Liberator*, dismissing them as insufficiently dedicated.

Public Response

Supporters of slavery were predictably outraged by the newspaper's message. Some Southerners burned copies of the paper, while others threatened violence if he continued to publish. Northern whites were not necessarily more supportive of Garrison's words. Though slavery had more or less been banned in the North by the time the *Liberator* began publishing, many Northerners of the 1830s were hardly abolitionists. Even in Boston, where antislavery sentiment was relatively strong, angry mobs threatened Garrison. Thus, in general, the public response to Garrison and the *Liberator* was as intense as the newspaper itself. Opinion was polarized; it seemed Garrison provoked either enthusiastic, wholehearted support or immediate hatred. There was little room for a middle ground.

During the years of the newspaper's publication, attitudes toward slavery began to harden in both the North and the South. By the 1850s, most Southerners had stopped apologizing for the drawbacks of the institution and argued instead

William Lloyd Garrison, who published The Liberator *for over thirty years.*

that slavery was a good and necessary system, better for blacks and whites alike than any other social and economic structure. There were many reasons for this less defensive stance, but certainly one of them was Garrison and his newspaper. The constant pressure from the *Liberator* forced the South into a more aggressive proslavery posture. At the same time, the *Liberator* was proof to some Southerners that Northerners were conspiring to undermine slavery and perhaps even provoke the slaves to revolt. The more Garrison thundered against slavery, the more suspicious the South grew of the North and its willingness to condone the Southern slavery system.

Partly in response, Northerners adopted an increasingly antislavery perspective over time. Even Northerners who did not care one way or the other about the welfare of blacks began to resent the South's single-minded determination to protect its way of life. Efforts to silence the *Liberator* made many Northern whites uncomfortable; they grew suspicious of the South and questioned its commitment to a Union in which the rights of all states were safeguarded. One by one reformers gave up on gradual emancipation plans, seeing the Southern unwillingness to compromise, and accepted proposals similar to Garrison's. Gradually, Northern abolitionist thought moved toward the *Liberator*'s positions.

The *Liberator* did not bring about the increasing division in opinion between North and South by itself. It was, however, an important reason for the split, and by extension for the Civil War and the ultimate end to slavery in the United States. The *Liberator*'s always principled, often courageous, and ultimately successful stand against slavery lifted this little newspaper out of obscurity and into the historical limelight. Even today, well over a century after it ceased publication, the *Liberator* is remembered and applauded for its accomplishments.

CHAPTER 1 Slavery and Abolition

No institution in American history has been as divisive, politically and socially, as slavery. Slavery set black against white, North against South, friend against friend. Even within groups of like-minded people, slavery sparked debate, and heated debate at that. Some slave owners preferred to think of slavery as a necessary evil, with an emphasis on the word *necessary*, while others championed it as a positive good. Similarly, some opponents of the system worked for an immediate and unconditional end to slavery, while others adopted a much more gradual approach. But the real proof of the divisive quality of slavery is this: In the end, the dispute over slavery led to the only civil war in U.S. history.

The first Africans in British North America came to Virginia in 1619, only twelve years after the first permanent British settlement was established at Jamestown. These men were probably not full-fledged slaves, however, but rather indentured servants; that is, workers pledged to their employer for a certain number of years. At first, slavery was slow to catch on among white Americans. By 1649, though slavery was legal in several colonies and a common practice in other parts of the world, few whites owned African American slaves. By one count, there were only about three hundred slaves in all of Virginia. Planters were content to use white laborers instead, typically bringing them from England as indentured servants.

That situation began to change, however, in the last decades of the seventeenth century. It became apparent to many white Americans that Africa was a source of truly cheap labor. There were biblical and cultural prohibitions against enslaving other white Europeans, but Africans were another matter altogether. Indeed, by selectively highlighting certain biblical passages and favorably interpreting others, it was possible to argue that the Bible justified the enslavement of blacks.

There was no doubt that white employers benefited economically by buying and owning slaves. An indentured servant might be paid very little, but an African could be paid nothing at all, except for the costs of cheap housing and poor food. An indentured servant might be forced to work for five or seven years, but the African's "contract" never ended. The only major cost to the slave owner was the initial price of purchase at auction.

The first Africans to arrive in British North America came to Virginia in 1619.

Thus, the scramble for slaves was on. By 1675, American ships were sailing for the African coast, ready to steal or buy another cargo of blacks for the colonial slave markets. Once in America, the unfortunate slaves were sold to the highest bidder and fated to a life of work, whether growing rice on a South Carolina low country plantation, cultivating tobacco for a Virginia farmer, or working as a domestic servant for a wealthy Boston couple. Throughout the South and in parts of the North, the white laborer was slowly replaced by the African slave.

North Versus South

Although slavery was at one time or another accepted by each of the original thirteen colonies, the institution became more and more localized as time went on. The most efficient use of slave labor soon proved to be on the large farms of the South. Crops such as rice and sugar required intensive, year-round labor. Thus, it made financial sense for planters to keep an army of workers always at the ready and on the premises.

In contrast, the less specialized, smaller farms of the North had less need for full-time help. The bulk of the work was in the spring and summer, and the work, even in season, tended to be less intensive and taxing than on Southern plantations. Rather than feed, house, and clothe African American slaves year-round, it was cheaper for these farmers to hire short-term laborers as required. At the same time, using slaves as domestic servants began to fall out of favor in the North. By 1759, only one of every ten American slaves lived north of Maryland.

Over the next few decades, the regional imbalance became even more pronounced. Despite the concerns voiced by Southern leaders such as Thomas Jefferson and George Washington, who did not entirely approve of slavery, the institution flourished in the South, especially after the development of the cotton gin in 1793. This invention, which efficiently separated the seeds, hulls, and other foreign material from cotton fibers, made large-scale cultivation of cotton possible across much of the South. Cotton growers could suddenly plant, harvest, and ship astonishing quantities of cotton—as long as they had ready labor at hand. Just as rice and sugar planters had found slave labor especially profitable, so too did the cotton growers. But while production of sugar and rice was limited geographically, cotton was grown across many Southern states. By 1800

A slave auction where prominent white land owners inspected the captives before purchasing them.

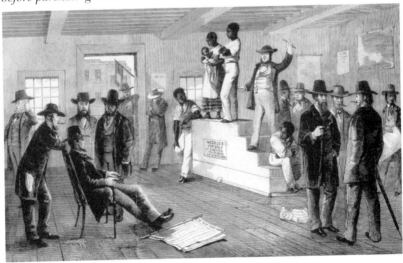

nearly two-thirds of all South Carolinians were slaves, and the populations of several other Southern states were at least half slave.

Meanwhile, the Northern colonies, whose economies were based on manufacturing, were moving in the opposite direction. Starting around the time of the American Revolution, Northern states began to limit or abolish slavery. Vermont banned slavery in 1777, Pennsylvania only a few years later. Most Northern states, including Rhode Island and New York, opted for a gradual emancipation plan in which slaves would be freed over a period of several years. The trend, however, was clear. Slavery was becoming an exclusively Southern institution.

Northern Attitudes Toward Slavery

History books often portray Northerners as united against slavery during the first half of the nineteenth century. This image is not accurate. While most Northerners of the 1830s had no great love for slavery, few were interested in abolishing it.

One reason for this tolerance was economic. North and South were tightly bound in complex business relationships. Cotton went north to Massachusetts textile mills; New York businessmen sold machinery and furniture to Southern plantations. Northern merchants, especially those who traded frequently in the South, saw arguments against slavery as potential threats to their businesses. They did not wish to offend the Southerners on whom their livelihoods depended. They also worried that changes in the slave system would interfere with Southern buying power and the production of cotton. "We can-

The invention of the cotton gin turned the time-consuming task of separating cotton seeds into a simple exercise.

Slaves prepare cotton on a Southern slave plantation.

not afford, sir, to let you and your associates succeed in your endeavor to overthrow slavery," one Northern merchant told antislavery leader Samuel May in 1835.[1]

Another reason was based on the American system of government, in which most laws were the province of the individual states. Most Northerners were uncomfortable meddling in another state's legal system and way of life. Much as they may have disliked slavery, they did not feel they had the right to dictate laws for other states. Northerners, wrote a Northern newspaper editor in 1836, "unanimously believe that there is no right in the general government to interfere with the plantation states in the management of their own slaves."[2]

But perhaps the strongest motive for Northern silence on slavery was racism. Even Northerners who disliked the notion of slavery were rarely friendly toward African Americans. Several states passed laws attempting to keep free blacks outside their borders altogether, and others severely restricted blacks' ability to hold jobs, own property, or vote. "The nation with all its institutions of right belong to the white men," a Connecticut town board concluded in 1833, opposing the opening of a school for African American girls.[3] Racism kept all but the most enlightened Northerners from advocating equal rights

The interior of a doubling room where women were forced to work long hours for very little pay.

for blacks. And racism also meant that few Northerners cared much about the fate of individual slaves.

Most Northerners also believed that if slavery were to end in the South, many former slaves were likely to come North in search of work. The newly freed slaves would be uneducated and extremely poor; that much was clear. They would be competing with Northern whites for jobs, thereby possibly putting local citizens out of work. And, if they were at all upset about their treatment as slaves, they might threaten, or even take, violent retribution. Fearing this on-slaught, many antislavery Northerners chose not to speak out strongly against the institution.

Gradual Emancipation

This ambivalence about slavery among Northerners had an inhibiting effect on those Northerners who did choose to speak out against the institution. In the first part of the nineteenth century, most antislavery Northerners adopted a relatively gentle tack. Rather than lam-basting the South for its evil ways, they tried to encourage enlightened reform, aiming their persuasive efforts at the more progressive slaveholders. Over and over again, the early abolitionists counseled patience. Far from insisting that all slaves be freed at once, they tended to argue instead for gradual emancipation, in which slavery would be phased out over time.

Gradual emancipation had worked before. Several Northern states had indeed abolished slavery over time. By passing laws and changing attitudes in one state after another, reformers had made it possible for slavery to be wiped out peacefully and without rancor. The South did present a more serious challenge, though, because of the sheer number of slaves, and also because of the degree to which the economy relied on slavery.

Various reformers suggested ways of achieving the goal of gradual emancipation for the South. Some suggested that all slave children

Northern Racism

On March 6, 1863, a white mob ran riot through central Detroit, attacking blacks and destroying their property. The flashpoint for the violence was a pair of crimes committed by a man the mob members believed was black. Without waiting for a trial, or even bothering to find out whether the man in question was actually African American (there is evidence that he was not), many Detroit citizens set out to hurt as many blacks as they could. This passage, excerpted from Branson and France's The Human Side of Afro-American History, *is an eyewitness account of the Detroit violence by a black man.*

> We were aroused by the yells of the mob, and, on going to the street, heard windows smashing and hammering against doors, with dreadful curses of "Kill the Nigger." A crowd rushed up to my residence and commenced their work of destruction in every possible way, with bricks, stones, and other destructive missiles, and the torch was soon set to our house. Myself and wife, with one child, had to make the best of our efforts to escape with our lives. They rushed after us with demoniac rage, and their curses and yells were terrifying. We would, most certainly, have fallen a prey to them, had not the hands [workers] in the Morocco Factory, just in the rear of our lot, called to us through there.

The family wandered three miles out of town, got lost, and ultimately spent the night in the woods. "Oh, Detroit! Detroit, how hast thou fallen!" the man mourned.

But the racism of Detroit was not much different from anywhere else in the North, and the riot was not unusual. Many other American cities suffered antiblack violence, both during and before the Civil War. The truth was that racism was sadly prevalent across the United States, not only in the South.

born after a certain date be declared free. Others preferred a plan in which all slave owners would be asked to release a certain percentage of slaves every year. A few argued that slave property be more heavily taxed, making it in the masters' interest to release their slaves. What nearly all reformers agreed on, however, was that gradual abolition was the best and most prudent approach. Slaveholders would only have to agree on a date by which slavery would be abolished, declared a Northern attorney. The exact date was not so important as the principle. "We will not quarrel as to a month, or a year, or twenty years," he added, so long as slavery would be eventually abolished.[4]

Consulting the South

Part of the appeal of gradual emancipation stemmed from the support many Southern leaders had given the idea since before the Revolution. Gradual emancipation was particularly popular in the upper South—the northern tier of slave states including Virginia, Kentucky, and Maryland. "I believe a time will come when an opportunity will be offered to abolish this lamentable Evil," Virginia patriot Patrick Henry wrote.[5]

Henry's sentiments were echoed by many other Southern leaders, from judges and generals to politicians. In the years after the Revolution, in fact, a number of well-known Southerners took their own counsel by freeing their slaves. Most only set their slaves free in their wills, but occasionally slaves were emancipated while their masters lived. As late as 1832, the subject of gradual emancipation came up for debate in the Virginia legislature. Though the proposal was ultimately defeated, the debate indicated the strength of the idea among at least some Southerners.

As a founding father of the United States, Patrick Henry was a known abolitionist.

Most abolitionists took these reform-minded Southerners quite seriously. They reasoned that it was foolish to attempt abolition without at least some support from the South. "Any plan of emancipation, to be effectual," wrote antislavery feminist Frances Wright, "must consult at once the pecuniary interests and prevailing opinions of the southern planters."[6] Plans that did not, Wright implied, were doomed to failure.

Exactly how sincere Southerners were about eliminating slavery was, of course, debatable. Certainly many Southerners at the turn of the century believed that they could not manage economically without their slaves. Many others saw no moral problem with slavery. Nevertheless, according to most reformers, gradual emancipation had a fair chance of being accepted by those who owned slaves. Insisting on immediate abolition, reformers reasoned, would never work; the South would only close ranks and ignore the abolitionists, and in the end any chance of eliminating slavery would be delayed if not destroyed. Thus, gradual abolition was the best of all possible emancipation plans.

Compensation and Colonization

To sweeten the pot for Southerners, early Northern abolitionists typically argued for two other items of interest to slaveholders: compensation and colonization. Compensation simply meant payment. Antislavery thinkers suggested that slave owners be paid for the slaves they set free. Whether funds were raised privately or came from the government, compensation, they believed, was only fair. After all, slaves represented a huge investment for wealthy plantation owners and small family farmers alike. It was not reasonable to expect a man to surrender his property and get nothing in return.

Colonization was a little more complicated. As mentioned, both Southerners and Northerners feared negative effects of releasing all slaves from bondage. The freed slaves, many whites argued, would be far from able to take their place in society; they would demand to be treated as citizens, however, whether they were "ready" for citizenship or not. This was a major concern. It was not right, one thinker warned, "that men should possess that freedom, for which they are entirely unprepared, and which can only prove injurious to themselves and others."[7] The effects, many whites believed, would be disastrous for everyone concerned.

As a result, many abolitionists recommended that freedom be combined with deportation. Slaves, once freed, would be shipped away from the United States, bound for Africa, Mexico, or the Caribbean. Colonization, as this plan was called, won support from progressive Southerners and antislavery Northerners alike. Colonization eliminated the fears whites had of marauding bands of free blacks tramping across the countryside, despoiling the land and menacing local families. The last drawback to freeing the slaves would be solved.

Indeed, plenty of Southerners applauded plans to deport the slaves. Some believed that it was truly the answer to the problem of slavery. "There are a number of slaveholders," said a Virginian in 1831, "who would voluntarily surrender their slaves, if the State would provide the means of colonizing them elsewhere."[8] Colonization, agreed a Kentucky minister, "has taught us how we may be relieved of the curse of slavery in a manner cheap, certain, and advantageous to both the parties."[9] Again, abolitionists enthusiastically sought this kind of Southern support. While not all Southerners were anxious to deport their slaves, many influential ones seemed open to the idea—enough, at any rate, for Northerners to believe that emancipation could succeed if linked to colonization.

Ready for Change

The abolition plans proposed by Northerners, then, had several characteristics. They relied on patience and evolution. They emphasized a gradual change of minds and attitudes rather than sweeping, immediate legislative change; their language was temperate and respectful, not loud and strident. The plans considered Southern slaveholders' ideas and needs. And finally, despite the schemes' lofty goals, their proponents were motivated to a greater or lesser degree by racism, by a desire to keep black people out of their lives and out of their nation.

But while Northern reformers were speaking gently and politely to the South, the South itself was changing its stance on slavery. By the 1830s there was a clear shift in the South's focus. Fewer Southern voices called for gradual emancipation. Even the promise of deportation did not seem to excite many slave owners. Instead, more and more slaveholders took the attitude that slavery was a positive force and a mark of a civilized culture. As they did so, the Northern abolitionists' goals began to appear less achievable and less rational.

Southern Attitudes

For years, echoing Washington, Patrick Henry, and others, Southerners had been defensive about slavery. It was not the best of all possible worlds, they admitted; perhaps, instead, it was just plain wrong. St. George Tucker, a Virginia judge, had this to say about his state's institution in 1796:

> Whilst America hath been the land of promise to Europeans, and their descendants, it hath been the vale of death to millions of the wretched sons of Africa. The genial light of liberty, which hath here shown with unrivalled lustre on the former, hath yielded no comfort to the latter, but to them hath proved a pillar of darkness. . . . Slavery [has been] ten

thousand times more cruel than the utmost extremity of those grievances and oppressions, of which we complained [during the American Revolution].[10]

Remarks like Tucker's were common before 1830. Many Southerners recognized the problems of slavery, and few were willing to call it a positive good.

By the time William Lloyd Garrison founded the *Liberator* in 1831, though, the new generation of Southerners had taken the offensive. Two quotations from the same Richmond newspaper are illuminating. In 1832 the paper editorialized that slavery was "a dark and growing evil." That sentiment was already a minority view, however; just over twenty years later the paper called slavery, instead, "a natural and necessary and . . . universal . . . institution of society."[11]

Southern apologists carried the argument to several fronts. To Northern concerns that slaves were brutalized, inhumanely treated, and unjustly stolen from their homelands, Southerners responded with flat denials. "The slaves are all well fed, well clad, have plenty of fuel, and are happy," wrote Virginian George Fitzhugh.[12] In fact, some argued, Southern slaves were considerably better off than most Northern "free" workers or European peasants. A Louisiana senator challenged anyone "to prove that the white laborers of the North are as happy, as contented, or as comfortable as the slaves of the South."[13] Unlike free workers, it was pointed out, the slave would be cared for in old age, and would never be out of work.

A slave "mammy" watches over the master's child.

Others presented supposedly scientific evidence that blacks were inferior to whites and ideally suited to a life of slavery. The bodies and brains of African Americans were measured and examined, and minor physical differences between whites and blacks were interpreted as evidence that the two were fundamentally different creatures, perhaps even different species. Social scientists, in turn, studied African culture and concluded that it was seriously backward compared with white civilizations. The intention was to prove that whites were superior. As less than fully equal (and perhaps less than fully human), blacks could not be expected to be capable of self-government. "There are, no doubt, many rights which belong to other men which are denied [the slave]," wrote a minister. "But is he fit to possess them?"[14] The answer, to the minister and to many other Southerners, was a clear "No."

The blacks' plight was said to be mitigated by contact with whites. "Nothing but arbitrary power," such as a slavemaster holds, wrote

In Defense of Slavery

Southern apologists for slavery argued that slavery was moral and just. The following excerpts are from a speech given by South Carolina governor George MacDuffie in 1835, as reprinted in William Dudley, Slavery. *MacDuffie's speech is a good example of Southern proslavery rhetoric during the years of the* Liberator.

"No human institution, in my opinion, is more manifestly consistent with the will of God than domestic slavery, and no one of His ordinances is written in more legible characters than that which consigns the African race to this condition, as more conducive to their own happiness, than any other of which they are susceptible. Whether we consult the sacred Scriptures or the lights of nature and reason, we shall find these truths as abundantly apparent as if written with a sunbeam in the heavens. Under both the Jewish and Christian dispensations of our religion, domestic slavery existed with the unequivocal sanction of its prophets, its apostles, and finally its great Author [that is, God]. . . .

That the African Negro is destined by Providence to occupy this condition of servile dependence is not less manifest. It is marked on the face, stamped on the skin, and evinced by the intellectual inferiority and natural improvidence of this race. They have all the qualities that fit them for slaves, and not one of those that would fit them for freemen. They are utterly unqualified, not only for rational freedom but for self-government of any kind. They are, in all respects, physical, moral, and political, inferior. . . . It is utterly astonishing that any enlightened American . . . should suppose it possible to reclaim the African race from their destiny."

philosopher S.A. Cartwright, "can restrain the excesses of [the slave's] animal nature."[15] In slaveholders' eyes, this civilizing influence justified the keeping of blacks in bondage. Slavery, the argument went, was in the slaves' own interest. The slave ships had given the African Christianity and the steadying hand of a kind and wise master. Left in the forests of Africa, blacks could never have progressed, slaveholders believed; in America, they might.

Still other Southerners looked to history and religion to justify their institution. "The patriarchs [Old Testament figures such as Abraham] themselves, those chosen instruments of God, were slaveholders," the governor of South Carolina pointed out in 1835. "No human institution . . . is more manifestly consistent with the will of God than domestic slavery."[16] The ancient Greeks held slaves, Southern defenders of the institution argued. So had the Romans. So, for that matter, had nearly every great culture in history. Indeed, the apologists continued, slavery had helped to make those cultures great, by allowing leisure time for the ruling class and increasing productivity.

Slave owners argued that every great culture, even the Greeks and Romans, owned slaves.

Whatever the reasoning, the conclusion was obvious. Slavery was a good system for everybody. Slaves, slaveholders, even non-slave-owning whites—all benefited from the South's institution. By the early 1830s the switch from an apologetic defense to an enthusiastic offense was well underway, and Southern resolve would only continue to stiffen and grow as the years went on.

This, then, was the background for William Lloyd Garrison's founding of the *Liberator*. Garrison began publishing his newspaper at a time when attitudes toward slavery were changing markedly in the South, and when the old ways of thinking about abolition were perceived as ineffective in the North. Between 1831 and 1865, the *Liberator* brought a new dimension to abolitionist sentiment. Moreover, it pushed both pro- and antislavery arguments in unexpected directions. Few other forums of its time were as integral in shaping attitudes on each side as the *Liberator* would prove to be.

CHAPTER 2

William Lloyd Garrison and the *Liberator*

William Lloyd Garrison is among the more controversial figures in American history. In his own time he was hated by many and loved by few. Some called him an extremely dangerous man whose ideas and methods deserved condemnation. Others thought of him as a great American and champion of human rights. Garrison's refusal to moderate his language, his near inability to compromise on any issue, and his steadfast devotion to a single cause won him instant friends or automatic scorn. "There shall be no neutrals," Garrison once said. "Men shall either like me or dislike me."[17]

Similarly, there have been few neutrals since Garrison's death. Different historians and different time periods have seen him in very different lights. Some have treated him as an inspired leader and a principled hero, even the single most important figure in the fight against slavery. Others have been more inclined to dismiss him as a footnote to history, a closed-minded man whose fury and venom did little to help the causes he supported.

Whether Garrison was hero or villain, humanitarian or rabble-rouser, one thing is clear: He was impossible to separate from the *Liberator*. For more than thirty years Garrison churned out issue after issue of the paper. There were occasional editorials signed by others, and Garrison frequently reprinted items from other newspapers for his readership. However, most of the words that appeared in the *Liberator* were Garrison's own. Even articles picked up from other papers usually included Garrison's own commentary. The *Liberator* was Garrison's brainchild. The connection between man and work was astonishingly close. To understand the newspaper and its place in history it is first necessary to understand Garrison himself.

Early Influences

Born in Newburyport, Massachusetts, in 1805, Garrison did not seem destined for a life of great achievement. He grew up poor and in unhappy family circumstances. His father abandoned the family when the boy was two, and his mother was often forced to leave the household in order to find or keep a job. Money was always tight. As a very young child, Garrison worked for a time delivering wood and selling candy on street corners. More than once he begged. As histo-

Garrison and Family Life

Unlike many other antislavery activists, Garrison had a full and rather happy family life. He married Helen Benson in 1834, and the couple had five sons and two daughters. Helen Garrison was a quiet but staunch supporter of William Lloyd's causes; she was particularly interested in women's rights. Some of the Garrisons' children took up the social reform work of their father, although not always in ways that entirely pleased him.

Garrison was remembered by his children as a kind and devoted father. His daughter Fanny recalled that she and her siblings were "drawn to him as if by a magnet," as quoted in Mayer, *All on Fire*, and that he treated them with "unbounded love." However, Garrison could not completely leave the *Liberator* out of his family life. When he once showed signs of withdrawing from his work in favor of spending time with a new baby, a friend chided him pointedly: "Your child—the *Liberator*—your eldest child, is suffering, as all children do, by the Father's absence." Garrison did come back to work. And his daughter Fanny recalled, as quoted in Cain's *William Lloyd Garrison*

and the Fight Against Slavery: Selections from the Liberator: "I was hardly more than an infant when my father came to my crib to give me a goodnight kiss. He said, 'What a nice warm bed my darling has! The poor little slave child is not so fortunate and is torn from its mother's arms. How good my darling ought to be!'"

Helen Benson, who married Garrison in 1834, was a staunch feminist and supporter of women's rights.

rian William Cain puts it, "These experiences left scars—and also compassion for outcasts."[18]

At the age of eight, young Garrison apprenticed himself to a shoemaker. One placement led to another, and before long he was working in a print shop. The work had its drawbacks. The shop smelled of ink, and the boy's hands were perpetually stained. But as Garrison learned how to set type and operate the printing press, he became intrigued with the process. More than that, Garrison became aware of the power of the printed word. Though he had had

Besides writing and editing the Liberator, *William Lloyd Garrison had the task of printing and typesetting.*

little schooling himself, he quickly saw that books, magazines, and handbills were excellent ways to spread opinions and ideas.

The newspaper, in particular, appealed to Garrison. As his master printer liked to say, the newspaper was "a most effective [vehicle] for disseminating literary, moral and religious instruction."[19] Garrison took this sentiment to heart. He spent much of his apprenticeship working for a local newspaper, the *Newburyport Herald*. By the age of twenty-one, when his apprenticeship ended, Garrison had made his career choice: He would be a newspaperman. Not just any news-paperman, however; instead, he would be joining "a new race of ed-itors," as he put it, by adopting a visionary outlook, working to make the world a better place, and giving his opinions as much as report-ing the news.[20]

Early Newspaper Experiences

Between 1826 and 1831, Garrison worked on several different news-papers in Massachusetts, Vermont, and Maryland. He composed type, reported the news, and—most important—wrote editorials. At each stop, Garrison gained valuable experience. He absorbed the subtleties of journalism, he gained practice in working with all kinds of people, and he took the time to read other publications.

At each stop Garrison also developed a stronger and shriller voice, especially on political matters. He wrote extensively on the issues of the day. Every Garrison-edited newspaper clearly revealed his beliefs. Often it was not necessary to read beyond the headlines to know which causes Garrison supported. Garrison opposed the use of liquor, for example; one of his newspapers bore the slogan "Moderate Drinking Is the Downhill Road to Intemperance and Drunkenness."[21] He distrusted governments, describing politics as a morally corrupt system in which the only rule was "You scratch my back, and I'll tickle your elbow."[22] Pacifism was another favorite topic of Garrison's early years: "I am conscientiously opposed to all military exhibitions," he informed his Vermont readers in 1828.[23]

But most of all, Garrison took up the antislavery cause during this time. Before 1826, abolitionism was just one of several ideals Garrison espoused. By 1829, however, it had risen to new prominence. "We give our pledge," he wrote that year, "that the liberation of the enslaved African shall always be uppermost in our pursuits."[24] Within a year, Garrison had left mainstream journalism to support the antislavery cause full-time, accepting the assistant editorship of a Baltimore-based abolitionist paper called the *Genius*. Garrison's concern for the fate of the slaves would never again take second place to any other issue.

Garrison's solutions to the slavery question changed during this time, too. At first, he was more or less aligned with the general currents of abolitionist sentiment. Like

Garrison, soon after the first publications of the Liberator.

his Baltimore employer, Quaker abolitionist Benjamin Lundy, Garrison began as a staunch gradualist and a believer in colonization. As late as July 1829, Garrison spoke at a Boston meeting in which he called immediate abolition "a wild vision." While his language was more strident than most antislavery thinkers of the period—in that same speech he described slavery as a "national sin" and added, "I tremble for the republic while slavery exists"—his ideas were not particularly unusual for his time.[25]

"Immediate and Complete Emancipation"

Within a year, however, unusual they were. By the time he arrived in Baltimore, Garrison's ideals had undergone a dramatic shift. "The slaves are entitled to immediate and complete emancipation," he wrote in his first issue of the *Genius*.[26] The more Garrison had considered the issues, the more he had come to the conclusion that fairness called for immediate emancipation. If slavery was wrong, he reasoned, then it should be stopped, and the sooner the better. No longer did Garrison accept the idea that immediate freedom was impractical. "The question of expedience has nothing to do with right," he argued, and what was right was immediate and unconditional freedom.[27]

Along with dropping his support for gradual abolition, Garrison also gave up on the doctrine of colonization. Certainly, the colonization movement was struggling. At a cost of thousands of dollars, only a few hundred blacks had been returned to Africa. Strictly from a logistical standpoint, it was becoming clear to Garrison that there were simply too many slaves to deport all of them, even if the will to do so were strong. "Altogether inadequate," he called colonization early in his Baltimore editorship.[28]

But Garrison also discovered that he opposed colonization on philosophical grounds. Most blacks, he reasoned, had been born in the United States, had helped to build the nation, and no longer had any ties to Africa. Thus, they were entitled to full citizenship. He was influenced in this also by the statements of a number of free blacks, who made it quite clear that they wished to stay. "[We] respectfully but firmly declare our determination not to participate in any part of [colonization]," wrote a group of black Philadelphians in 1817.[29] Garrison, unlike many of his contemporaries, trusted the blacks to make this choice.

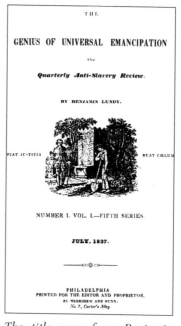

The title page from Benjamin Lundy's The Genius of Universal Emancipation.

Thus, within a period of only a few months, Garrison had changed course on the issue of slavery. He had been a vocal but cautious opponent of slavery and the slave system, indistinguishable from most abolitionists of the time. Now his ideas had moved far from the mainstream; they were unacceptable not only to Southerners but to many antislavery Northerners as well. And Garrison's shrill, even vicious attacks on slaveholders continued. In one celebrated example from 1829, Garrison described the owner of a slave-trading ship and its captain as "highway robbers and murderers" who should "BE SENTENCED TO SOLITARY CONFINEMENT FOR LIFE."[30] The ship owner sued him for libel and won the case; Garrison spent several weeks in the Baltimore jail as a consequence.

Prominent clergyman Lyman Beecher admired Garrison's efforts, but deemed them a waste of time.

An Insignificant Mechanic

In 1830, Garrison returned to Boston, where he delivered antislavery lectures and lobbied others likely to support his cause. These included abolitionist churchmen, philanthropists, politicians, and merchants. Unfortunately for Garrison, however, he was not terribly successful at drumming up support. Many of these abolitionists continued to call for gradual emancipation with colonization, and Garrison found himself treated as an outsider.

A few of those Garrison approached were downright rude, such as the minister who called him a "low-lived, ignorant, insignificant mechanic."[31] More typical, however, was the response of prominent clergyman Lyman Beecher. Beecher said he admired Garrison's enthusiasm, but told Garrison to "give up his fanatical notions" regarding colonization and gradual abolition. Garrison, Beecher condescendingly admitted, could still be helpful to the antislavery cause if he agreed to "be guided by us"—that is, by the recognized church leaders of the city.[32] Beecher's response was standard. The rich and powerful of Boston were not ready to listen to Garrison's message.

A handful of Bostonians, however, were ready. Most obvious among these was Boston's small black community. Garrison's speeches were well attended and received by the eighteen hundred or so free African Americans who had settled in Boston. At a time when even the most liberal of thinkers, like Beecher, were counseling patience in the struggle against slavery, these men and women found it exciting to hear Garrison attack slavery directly. "We had good enough doctrine [i.e., philosophy] before Garrison," one black Bostonian admitted later, "but we wanted a good example."[33] Another local African American spoke for many when he praised Garrison as a man "full of virtue and consolation."[34]

Support came from other quarters. A Connecticut minister named Samuel May heard Garrison speak and was much moved. "I am not sure that I can endorse all you have said this evening," he told Garrison after the speech, "but I am sure you are called to a great work, and I mean to help you."[35] Two young lawyers were convinced as well. The three offered financial help and—equally important—their good reputations; while none had the stature of a Beecher or a political leader such as Daniel Webster, each was respected and could lend Garrison's campaign some needed prestige.

Connecticut minister Samuel May became an early supporter of Garrison and his ideas.

With this support, Garrison decided that the time was ripe for his dream: establishing a newspaper devoted to immediate emancipation for all the slaves. He would act as editor, with the help of his good friend Isaac Knapp. The foreman of a local print shop allowed Garrison to use his shop's presses until Garrison could afford one of his own. Other friends offered to serve as agents for the newspaper, selling subscriptions and soliciting donors. Throughout the fall of 1830, Garrison planned, organized, and wrote. On January 1, 1831, the first edition of the *Liberator* was produced.

The *Liberator*

By today's standards, the *Liberator* was unimpressive indeed. Each issue was printed on a single sheet of newsprint, folded over once, yielding four printed pages, each about the size of a sheet from a legal pad. (In 1837, the size was increased to 16 **x** 23 inches, slightly larger than a sheet of newspaper today, but the number of pages remained the same.) A weekly from the start, the paper attracted few early subscribers. Even after two years there were only about two hundred white subscribers, many of them personal friends of Garrison's. Cir-

Newspapers

In Garrison's time, newspapers were not just in the business of objective reporting of the news; they were also expected to give opinions. In this way, the *Liberator* was not entirely different from other newspapers of its day. Quite a few papers of the 1830s and 1840s, for instance, were closely connected with a political party to an extent almost unknown today. Garrison himself worked for an avowedly Federalist newspaper at one point. Nor was evenhandedness in news coverage valued the way it is now. On the contrary, readers often chose a paper specifically because of its political leanings.

The newspaper business, in general, was a good deal more freeflowing in the 1830s than it is now. Without radio, television, or computers, newspapers were critically important in spreading information and opinions. While today only a few very large American cities have more than one daily newspaper, in Garrison's time even small cities had two, three, or even more. Many of these were not that different in format from the *Liberator*: small, two- or three-man operations that printed issues of four or eight pages. Some were even less impressive: fly-by-night organizations that published irregularly and closed up shop without warning.

Even Garrison's propensity for insult and outrage was somewhat in tune with the times, though he still shocked many more people than did the average editor. A sampling of quotations from the period of the *Liberator*'s publication demonstrates that he was far from the only one who lambasted his opponents. These excerpts appear in Herbert Mitgang's *Lincoln as They Saw Him* and Stephen Bates's *If No News, Send Rumors*:

The *New York Times* called rival editor Horace Greeley "Old Satanic."

The *Rocky Mountain News* ran a picture of a donkey's rear with the caption "A life-like portrait of the sensitive editor of the [*Rocky Mountain*] *Herald*. Copyright secured."

The *Chicago Times* summed up an 1858 debate involving Abraham Lincoln as follows: "Lincoln's Heart Fails Him!/Lincoln's Legs Fail Him!/Lincoln's Tongue Fails Him!/Lincoln's Arms Fail Him!/LINCOLN FAILS ALL OVER!!/The People Refuse to Support Him!/The People Laugh at Him!"

In 1862, with the Civil War in full swing, the *Richmond Enquirer* questioned whether Lincoln should most appropriately be called "coward, assassin, savage, [or] murderer of women and babies?" and concluded that the best name would be "Lincoln, the Fiend."

After Lincoln's assassination in 1865, the *Tri-Weekly Telegraph* of Houston faintly condemned the killer but added, "From now until God's judgment day, the minds of men will not cease to thrill at the killing of Abraham Lincoln."

culation among blacks was higher, but circulation never exceeded three thousand, and the newspaper rarely broke even financially.

But Garrison had a secret weapon: himself. He thought, breathed, and lived immediate abolition. His entire life, it seemed, was given

A typical page from the Liberator *newspaper.*

over to the *Liberator*. He worked part-time jobs during the day to earn enough to put out the *Liberator* at night. He tirelessly sought out subscribers and donors; friends who did not share his passion were ignored. For a time he lived on nothing but bread, milk, and fruit, and he sometimes had to sleep in his office. For Garrison, however, the sacrifices and hardships were necessary to speed the cause of abolition, and he never complained. In the end, the newspaper lasted through thirty-five years of publication, during which time Garrison missed not a single issue.

While Garrison had help in putting the *Liberator* together, he was quite certainly in charge of the operation. Garrison, and usually Garrison alone, decided what material would make up each week's issue. As a rule, the paper was a hodgepodge of original editorials and articles taken from other publications. Reprinting other editors' articles was a common practice of the time, and Garrison made frequent use of it. The pieces he reprinted included descriptions of slavery and antislavery efforts; Garrison also reprinted editorials supporting or opposing his own positions. As a rule, Garrison added his own commentary to reprints, which sometimes exceeded the length of the original piece.

Once the content was determined, production began. The paper had to be set in type, with about one hundred thousand characters per issue and no machines to help sort and place the letters. The blank newsprint was then inked, dried, collated, bundled, and sent out to subscribers. Of all the aspects of running a newspaper, Garrison said that the mechanical work required "the most unremitted labor."[36] Garrison did prove somewhat more willing to allow help with this part of the process than he did with the editorial duties of the *Liberator*. Still, he often worked late at night composing type with the help of a single assistant.

Content

From the outset, the *Liberator* championed immediate abolition. The name of the paper suggested its bias. So did nearly all the articles and editorials. The first issue featured a poem by Garrison in which he described the *Liberator's* mission with these words:

> My task is hard—for I'm charged to save
> *Man from his brother!*—to redeem the slave![37]

Garrison's first task was to separate himself from the gradualists and the supporters of colonization. This he did in characteristically strong language. Gradualism, he thundered, was both unfair and doomed to failure. As he wrote early in his career at the helm of the *Liberator*:

I utterly reject, as delusive and dangerous in the extreme, every plea which justifies a procrastinated [delayed] and an indefinite emancipation, or which concedes to a slave owner the right to hold his slaves as *property* for any limited period, or which contends for the gradual preparation of the slaves for freedom.[38]

"Delusive and dangerous" were strong words indeed, but Garrison was just getting warmed up.

The *Liberator* took the same strong stance against colonization schemes. In harsh words Garrison continually registered his disapproval of those who would return blacks to Africa. Colonization, the *Liberator* argued, was "wrong in principle and impotent in design."[39] The editorial stance of the newspaper was clear: African Americans had earned the right to stay in America if they chose.

Susan B. Anthony, women's rights activist of the 1800s.

But Garrison went further. Along with the *Liberator*'s antislavery stand, the newspaper increasingly supported extending ordinary rights of citizenship to blacks. A *Liberator* editorial addressed the slaves as "Brethren and countrymen," a title not often used by whites of the time.[40] "I assert their perfect equality with ourselves, as part of the human race," he stated in 1842.[41] Over and over, Garrison argued that the ignorance of slaves was a result of their servitude, not an inborn quality. "Treat them like rational beings, and you may surely expect rational treatment in return," he wrote.[42]

Antiviolence and Antigovernment

Although immediate abolition was the focus of the *Liberator*, Garrison pushed constantly for other ideals, too, just as he had in his earlier positions. Women's rights were a favorite issue. The *Liberator* often editorialized in favor of women's participation on abolitionist committees and in antislavery work. Religion was another recurrent topic. Garrison did not formally belong to any church. He considered himself a spiritual man, but believed organized religion to be confining, legalistic, and unwilling to stand up for what was right. The pages of the *Liberator* were filled with attacks on clergymen whom Garrison considered "foes of God and man" as well as general condemnation of churches. Christianity in New England, he charged, had been taken over by an "oath-taking, war-making, man-enslaving religion."[43]

Another important ideal of Garrison's was pacifism. Through most of the *Liberator*'s history, the newspaper staunchly supported change by moral force, rather than by physical power. "We register our testimony, not only against all wars, whether offensive or defensive," Garrison wrote in 1838, "but [against] all preparations for war."[44] Nevertheless, Garrison argued, it was the duty of any moral person to protest immoral actions by governments or other citizens. However, this protest could not take the form of violence, and those he called nonresistants should expect to pay the penalty for breaking laws, even unjust ones.

Admittedly, Garrison's pacifist resolve was often stretched. While he condemned slave revolts, he could not resist indirect approval of slaves who did rise up against their masters. "We say, that the possibility of a bloody insurrection at the South fills us with dismay," he wrote in the *Liberator*'s second issue. "We avow, too, as plainly, that if any people were ever justified in throwing off the yoke of their tyrants, the slaves are that people."[45] Nevertheless, the *Liberator* spoke forcefully in favor of pacifism until the start of the Civil War.

Along with a tendency toward nonviolence came a deep distrust of government. "We cannot acknowledge allegiance to any human government," Garrison wrote in 1838.[46] Garrison saw politics as fatally flawed. "Political action is not moral action," he argued.[47] Political action relied on a majority, on lobbying, and on laws, while moral action relied instead on the changing of attitudes from within.

Indeed, Garrison saw few differences among political parties and political leaders. To him moderate Southerners, staunch defenders of slavery, and abolitionists not as radical as Garrison himself were all enemies, plain and simple. Garrison did not urge readers to run for elective office or to support particular candidates. In fact, the *Liberator* often advised its readers that voting itself was immoral, for voting meant taking part in an immoral government.

As was true of pacifism, the antigovernment streak in Garrison's thought waxed and waned. More

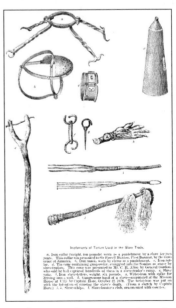

Implements of Torture Used in the Slave Trade.

Implements of torture used in the slave trade.

than once he advocated political action. "Secession from the government is a religious and political duty," he argued in 1844, encouraging non-slaveholders to separate peacefully from the rest of the nation. "Our motto is, 'NO UNION WITH SLAVEHOLDERS.'"[48] Though his suspicions of political leaders and parties began to mellow toward the time of the Civil War, for most of the *Liberator's* existence distrust of government was a common theme.

Tone

Important as the *Liberator's* content was, its tone was equally significant. To Garrison, there was no virtue in compromise or in an attempt to understand another's perspective. "WE ARE IN THE RIGHT," he thundered in 1844.[49] As a result, Garrison was a fierce and uncompromising writer. He said what he meant, regardless of who might be offended, and he refused to sugarcoat his words. "I do not wish to think, or speak, or write, with moderation," he proclaimed in the first issue of the *Liberator*. "I am in earnest—I will not equivocate—I will not excuse—I will not retreat a single inch—AND I WILL BE HEARD."[50]

During the life of the *Liberator*, Garrison regularly used biting sarcasm and barely contained anger to lambast slavery. "Sins the most flagrant," Garrison called the institution in 1832, "conduct the most cruel . . . acts the most oppressive!"[51] These were not the words of a moderate gently urging the South to mend its ways. Nor did calling slavery "a root of bitterness, which is poisoning the whole nation," endear him to slaveholders.[52] Garrison peppered his text with words like "bloody," "wicked," and "brutal" in virtually every issue of the *Liberator*. Even so, Garrison believed that words were not sufficient. "The whole scope of the English language is inadequate to describe the horrors and impieties of slavery," he wrote.[53]

Garrison used similar venom on his opponents. "Patriotic hypocrites!" he called slave owners. "Treasonable disunionists!"[54] It was not necessary to be a slaveholder, nor even in favor of the slave system, to be subject to these insults. Kentucky senator Henry Clay, a colonization advocate, was described as "a pitiable object" and "an awful curse." Massachusetts politician Daniel Webster, who ran afoul of Garrison by supporting a compromise on slavery, was "lick spittle of the slavehold[ers]."[55] Garrison even lit into runaway slave turned abolitionist Frederick Douglass when Douglass disagreed with him on several issues, calling Douglass dishonest and inconsiderate.

And Garrison took on institutions, too, in the same boiling tones of outrage. The American Colonization Society, he wrote, was based on "fear and selfishness."[56] Churches that refused to stand for immediate emancipation were "clotted with innocent blood."[57] He attacked the Constitution literally, by burning it in public, and metaphorically, in the pages of the *Liberator*. "A covenant with death," he called it, "an agreement with hell."[58] The Union itself fared no better. "Accursed be it," he wrote in 1845, "as a libel on Democracy, and a bold assault on Christianity!"[59]

Much of what Garrison wrote was shocking to the general public, in tone and style if not in content. That was, in fact, Garrison's intention. In part, the strident words were the result of Garrison's own deep-seated feelings on slavery and his certainty that he was right. Asked by Samuel May why he seemed perpetually "all on fire," Garrison replied, "Brother May, I have need to be all on fire, for I have mountains of ice about me to melt."[60] The evils of slavery justified harsh language.

Daniel Webster, referred to by Garrison as "lick spittle of the slaveholders," supported a compromise on slavery.

But Garrison also meant to provoke and irritate. "My language . . . will displease many, I know," he wrote. "To displease them is my intention."[61] Garrison wanted his newspaper to stand out from the rest of the crowd, and so he chose not to use a measured tone. He reasoned, perhaps accurately, that his writings could affect more people by being controversial.

Moreover, Garrison liked to see himself as a gadfly, taking up unpopular causes in unpopular ways. He was never happier than when facing long odds and public disapproval. "We shall be ridiculed as fools," he announced proudly in one document, "scorned as visionaries, branded as disorganizers, reviled as madmen, threatened and perhaps punished as traitors."[62] Garrison saw himself as well outside the mainstream and thrived on that image. Hostile and sarcastic language toward everyone else was a good way to reinforce his outsider status.

As Garrison went, so went the *Liberator*. The more Garrison saw himself as a rebel and a truthful voice crying unheard in the wilderness, the more the *Liberator* reflected that view. As Garrison eventually modified his ideas on nonviolence and government, so too did the *Liberator*. Garrison married and had children, but the great love of his life may well have been the newspaper. Without Garrison's unique character, style, and voice, the *Liberator* could not have accomplished all that it did.

Chapter 3 Philosophy

The concerns of the *Liberator* were many. Though the *Liberator* is best known today for its work against slavery, Garrison's stances on other issues were important too. Garrison campaigned tirelessly for nonviolent resistance and against a reliance on government, for fair treatment of women and blacks, and for the power of moral leadership in addition to his battle for immediate abolition. Moreover, these side issues reveal much of the thinking and philosophy that made the *Liberator* what it was.

"Let Other Subjects Alone"

Garrison's support for various social issues was controversial, even among his friends. Some abolitionists complained that the *Liberator* was dividing the antislavery movement by bringing up civil rights, antigovernment thinking, or the roles of women. Indeed, the movement did split several times over precisely these issues, with "political" and "moral" abolitionists going their separate ways and estrangement between supporters and opponents of women's participation. Other friends fretted that continued emphasis on subjects other than slavery would alienate the great mass of sympathetic Northerners who might accept Garrison's thinking on abolition but not his criticism of, for example, government. Garrison was forever receiving advice from supporters to stop talking so loudly about certain topics. "Still do I beg of you, brother," a friend wrote him in 1837, "to let other subjects alone until slavery is finished."[63]

Yet Garrison did not stop. Not until the last few years of his career with the *Liberator* did he begin to relax his stands on governments and violence, and even then he was far from a full-fledged supporter of either. In the same way, civil rights and tolerance, both for blacks and for women, were uppermost in the pages of the *Liberator* for many years. No doubt, Garrison supported these causes in part because they were unpopular, and he enjoyed being a gadfly. In part, too, he continued writing his opinions on these issues because he resented being asked to drop them; just as stubborn children might do something precisely because their parents tell them not to, Garrison delighted in confounding friends as well as enemies.

But it would be a mistake to read too much importance into Garrison's desire to be different and provocative. Garrison also acted out of deep philosophical convictions. According to his ideals, he could not conscientiously abandon any of these causes. Instead, Garrison believed that all his goals were closely connected, with abolitionism at the heart of everything. "The scope of Anti-Slavery is boundless," he wrote in an 1859 editorial. "There is nothing which pertains to the intellect, heart, soul, or interests of man that is not wrapped up in this movement."[64] Abolitionism, central as it was, was only one part of a grander philosophy that would encompass and promote the highest virtues.

The connections were sometimes obvious, sometimes less clear. A movement that freed slaves, the *Liberator* stressed again and again, was of little moral or ethical value if it then returned the slaves to Africa, or kept them in America as second-class citizens. Thus, to Garrison, abolition and civil rights were very nearly one and the same. Similarly, slavery was inherently violent, because the slaves were held in bondage through the use of force. They were beaten to make them work, which was violent, and they had been kidnapped into slavery to begin with, which was violent as well. Thus, to Garrison, opposition to slavery necessarily implied support for pacifism, for violence permitted slavery to begin, to grow, and to flourish.

Moreover, Garrison's ideals were heavily influenced by many different sources. Pacifism, antigovernment sentiment, rights for freed slaves—all had a long and honorable intellectual history, even if they did not dominate American thought of the time. The *Liberator* cited many of Garrison's precursors approvingly during the course of its thirty-five years, filtered, of course, through the editor's individual perspective. Garrison tended to pick out kernels of wisdom from various sources and traditions, discarding the rest in a way that might not have pleased the original sources. And, ever the zealot, Garrison turned even the simplest, gentlest of ideals into loud, confrontational manifestos. But that willingness to experiment, to rethink, and to reformulate old philosophies was part of what made the *Liberator* unique.

A Passion for Reading

Garrison had little formal schooling, but that did not prevent him from learning on his own. In his late teens and early twenties he read voraciously, devouring book after

The verses of British Romantic poet Lord Byron inspired Garrison to more emotional pleas for the immediate emancipation of all slaves.

book in all genres and disciplines. He was especially excited by the verses of the British Romantic poet Lord Byron, who often wrote of heroes who were outcasts from society. "He who surpasses or subdues mankind," Byron wrote in *Childe Harold's Pilgrimage*, "must look down on the hate of those below." Those were lines Garrison would come to understand as the clamor against the *Liberator* rose.

Garrison also appreciated Byron's emotionalism and the drama in his poems. He once wrote that Byron was better than anyone else at "rousing the blood like a trumpet call."[65] No editor, in turn, was better than Garrison at doing exactly the same, and it is not hard to understand Byron's influence and appeal to the impressionable young Garrison.

Garrison also read less intense poetry. He was fond of the works of Victorians such as Felicia Hemans, a British writer all but forgotten today. One of Hemans's few famous verses, "Casabianca," tells of a boy who refuses to leave a burning ship until his father, the captain, gives him permission. Permission never comes because, unknown to the boy, the father is already dead. The boy never wavers, however, going down with the ship. Hemans applauds the boy's courage and his willingness to do what he thinks is right. "The noblest thing which perished there," Hemans wrote to close "Casabianca," "was that young faithful heart."[66] From this and other Hemans poems, Garrison took away a conviction that doing what was right was important, no matter the consequences. There was something noble and heroic about dying for an ideal.

Garrison also worked his way through Shakespeare's plays and the novels of popular writers of the time, such as Sir Walter Scott, best remembered for *Ivanhoe*. He also read and enjoyed the works of religious novelists who, as he put it, gave "instruction in the dress of innocent amusement."[67] While the *Liberator* rarely printed much "innocent amusement," the goal of instruction was dear to Garrison's heart, and it is easy to see the influence of these education-oriented novelists on Garrison's later career.

Whatever he read, Garrison read carefully and thoughtfully. As a young adult, he began a literary society and encouraged his friends to join. Garrison was determined to make up for his lack of early education. Though he never mastered some of the subjects that a typical college student of the time would have encountered, Garrison nevertheless became a solidly well-read adult. The books he encountered along the way helped to establish his overall philosophy.

The Bible

The book Garrison prized above all others, and which defined his ideas more than any other, was the Bible. Although Garrison quarreled frequently with organized religion, he thought of himself as a deeply religious man, and the pages of the *Liberator* were filled with biblical references. Much of Garrison's antislavery rhetoric, for instance, rested on biblical grounds, and his ideas on pacifism and government were frequently supported by biblical examples as well. "[I will] consult no statute-book other than THE BIBLE," he thundered at one point, and similar sentiments often echoed in the pages of the *Liberator*.[68]

Slaveholding Southerners also quoted the Bible extensively in their attempt to justify their institution. The Old Testament was especially useful for Southern thinkers. Servants from other nations "shall be your possession," Leviticus 25 instructed the Hebrews. "And ye shall take them as an inheritance for your children after you, to inherit them for a possession; they shall be your bondmen for ever." Such verses satisfied Southern slaveholders that God was on their side.

Garrison, however, rejected this attitude completely. His biblical reference point was the New Testament, not the jealous, omniscient, and somewhat vengeful God of the ancients, but the gentle, turn-the-other-cheek mentality of Jesus Christ. To be sure, Garrison took from Christianity what made sense to him and abandoned the rest. Many Christian ministers of his time took issue as much with his theology as with his style of presentation, or with the fact that he rarely attended church. Yet Garrison himself was secure in his Christian beliefs, and without the Bible the *Liberator* would have been a very different newspaper altogether.

"Come, Come, Lord Jesus"

The Bible's influence on Garrison began with its stance on slavery. Of course, the mentions of slavery in the Old Testament were nearly all unfavorable to his position, so Garrison looked to the New Testament for support of abolition. Though the Gospels had nothing specific to say about freeing slaves, Garrison nevertheless believed that the spirit of the New Testament represented a strong condemnation of slavery. To Garrison, the New Testament superseded the Old; Jesus Christ had wiped out the old legalistic codes of conduct and replaced them with a more humane "higher law"—the rule of conscience and of moral right.[69] "According to the law of God," Garrison could therefore write, slavery was "null and void from the beginning."[70]

As described in the Bible, Garrison noted, Jesus spoke up for the downtrodden of society: the sick, the social outcasts, and the servants, among others. Surely, he reasoned, this benevolence extended to slaves. "Come, come, Lord Jesus," he cried during a New York City speech, "come quickly, and bind up the broken-hearted, and set the captive free!"[71]

The theme Garrison drew from the Gospels was one of love and kindness. Jesus, the *Liberator* repeated again and again, demanded certain loving and caring behaviors from his followers. "The moral precepts of the Bible are diametrically opposed to slavery," maintained New England minister Francis Wayland, a college president and contemporary of Garrison's. "They are, Thou shalt love thy neighbor as thyself, and all things whatsoever ye would that man should do unto you, do ye even so unto them."[72] Though Garrison did not accept everything Wayland said, he agreed heartily with this observation. The Golden Rule was paramount in Christianity, and slavery surely violated that principle.

Taken together, these interpretations led Garrison directly to a philosophy of antislavery. Slaveholders could not possibly be obeying Jesus' command, he wrote, since they would never agree to change places with those they enslaved. Nor could any person truly love someone whom he held in bondage. The notion that slaveholders and their allies called themselves Christians was, to Garrison, a terrible perversion of biblical ideals. "The Gospel of Peace and Mercy preached by him who steals, buys and sells the purchase of the Messiah's blood!"

In an attempt to incite better treatment of slaves, the teachings of Jesus Christ were a typical topic of the Liberator.

he wrote sarcastically in an early issue of the *Liberator*.[73]

The Gospels, too, opposed such halfway measures as colonization and gradual emancipation; at least, such was Garrison's reading of them. "Sentiments more hostile to the spirit of the Gospel," he wrote about colonization schemes, "cannot be found."[74] Jesus, he was sure, would have Americans move against slavery both quickly and decisively. "We would be filled with the spirit of CHRIST," he announced; "we purpose, in a moral and spiritual sense, to speak and act boldly in the cause of GOD."[75] If God favored emancipation, as Garrison believed, then waiting and compromise was wrong, and immediate action was called for.

Pacifism

The Bible also influenced the *Liberator*'s pacifism. Once again Garrison took the New Testament as his guide. The *Liberator* frequently quoted the passages in which Christ advocates nonviolence. "Ye have heard that it hath been said, An eye for an eye, and a tooth for a tooth," counsels Matthew 5:38–39, a favorite of Garrison's. "But I say unto you, That ye resist not evil: but whosoever shall smite thee on thy right cheek, turn to him the other also." Citing passages such as these, Garrison argued for nonresistance. "The penal code of the old covenant [i.e., the Old Testament]," Garrison announced in 1838, "has been abrogated by JESUS CHRIST."[76]

The *Liberator*'s pacifist tendencies ran deep. Garrison found it hard to condemn those who used force for abolition, but he was clearly troubled by the poor fit of violence with Jesus' words. "In the name of God," Garrison wrote after Northern abolitionist John Brown tried to free the slaves by violent rebellion, "I . . . disarm John Brown, and every slave at the South."[77] Elijah Lovejoy, an abolitionist editor killed by a mob, "was certainly a martyr," Garrison admitted. Nonetheless, since Lovejoy had used weapons in self-defense, Garrison continued, "strictly speaking—he was not . . . a Christian martyr."[78]

"After the Pattern of Christ"

Similarly, Garrison supported his distrust of government with references to the Bible. "We recognize but one KING and LAWGIVER, one JUDGE and RULER of mankind," Garrison wrote.[79] He saw Jesus as a peaceful revolutionary who urged his followers to look not to governments but to a higher law. In Garrison's eyes, Jesus instructed Christians to obey earthly laws so far as they were able, but not to trust in government for solutions: It was the kingdom of heaven, not the kingdoms of the earth, that mattered. "We shall submit to every ordinance of man, FOR THE LORD'S SAKE," Garrison wrote; "obey all the requirements of Government, except such as we deem contrary to the commands of the Gospel."[80]

Governments were human institutions, and, like all institutions, were all too easily corrupted. Garrison saw dozens of examples of that every day: preachers who forever counseled gradualism, politicians unwilling to take on "slave power," men who voted without thinking through all the issues. However, the root of Garrison's antigovernment sentiment came from the Bible. If Jesus spoke suspiciously of politics and laws, then Garrison was suspicious of them as well.

Indeed, what Garrison gleaned from the Bible went even deeper than the ideas of abolition, pacifism, and antigovernment. The Bible gave him his persona. He patterned himself after Jesus, and wrote of himself in the *Liberator* in the same terms. Taking up the cause of abolition, he warned his followers, "may subject us to insult, outrage, suffering, yea, even death itself. . . . Tumults may arise against us. The ungodly and violent . . . may combine to crush

Thomas Paine

The figure in early American history most like Garrison is arguably Thomas Paine. Like Garrison, Paine, a Revolutionary War pamphleteer, held strong opinions and circulated them; like Garrison, Paine's opinions were considered quite radical even by many of those who agreed with him in general outline; and like Garrison, Paine's ideas spoke to concepts of universal freedom and natural rights. Both were humanitarian reformers who were influenced by Quaker thought. And Paine, too, was no friend to slavery: he once called it "the most horrid of all traffics," as quoted in David Powell's *Tom Paine: The Greatest Exile.*

Paine's language, too, was much the same as Garrison's. Both men minced no words and seemed to have no doubts about the rightness and justice of their cause. Paine was more accepting of war and politics than was Garrison. Nevertheless, many of Paine's writings could easily have come from Garrison's pen as well. Except for the reference to war, this is an excellent example:

We fight not to enslave, but to set a country free, and to make room upon the earth for honest men to live in. In such a case we are sure we are right; and we leave to you [a British general to whom the lines are addressed] the despairing recollection of being the tool of a miserable tyrant.

Oddly, however, references to Paine in the *Liberator* were rare. Garrison evidently did not see himself as influenced in any way by Paine, and few historians have drawn a strong link between the two.

COMMON SENSE;

ADDRESSED TO THE

INHABITANTS

OF

A M E R I C A,

On the following interesting

S U B J E C T S.

I. Of the Origin and Design of Government in general, with concise Remarks on the English Constitution.

II. Of Monarchy and Hereditary Succession.

III. Thoughts on the present State of American Affairs.

IV. Of the present Ability of America, with some miscellaneous Reflections.

Man knows no Master save creating HEAVEN, Or those whom choice and common good ordain.

THOMSON.

PHILADELPHIA;

Printed, and Sold, by R. BELL, in Third-Street,

MDCCLXXVI.

Thomas Paine's pamphlet Common Sense *sparked America to rebel against England.*

44

Making emotional links between Jesus and emancipation, Garrison hoped to cause others to reconsider their views of slavery.

us. So they treated the MESSIAH, whose example we are humbly striving to emulate."[81]

Garrison saw himself as a gentle prophet, who spoke nothing but the truth, helped the lowest of the low, and was killed for his efforts. "Ours must be a bloodless strife," he wrote, "excepting our blood be shed."[82] More than once he wrote of the possibility that he would be murdered, and it is easy to detect a subtle wish for martyrdom in his philosophy. But he also saw himself as the righteous Jesus, the man who threw the moneychangers from the temple and angrily rebuked the rich and powerful. "The more peaceable a man becomes, after the pattern of Christ," he wrote in 1838, "the more he is inclined to make a disturbance, to be aggressive, to 'turn the world upside down.'"[83]

The Society of Friends

For the most part, religious thinkers of Garrison's time had little influence on the *Liberator*. Because Garrison rejected much of mainstream Christian thought, preachers like Lyman Beecher were not sufficiently revolutionary or apolitical to suit him, and in any case Garrison preferred the words of the Gospels without dogmatic interpretation.

Garrison did make an exception, however, for one religious group: the Society of Friends, popularly known as Quakers. Much of Garrison's philosophy was very much in tune with Quaker thought of the time. The Friends upheld pacifism in almost all contexts, which attracted Garrison. Even self-defense was forbidden among many Friends. So it was for the *Liberator*. "I deny the right of any people to *fight* for liberty," Garrison wrote once, "and so far am a Quaker in principle."[84] Similarly, Friends were among the leading American practitioners of nonresistance and the notion that governments ought to be disobeyed if laws conflicted with a higher ethical idea.

Though Garrison despised mainstream religion, he often made exceptions for his friend Benjamin Lundy and other Quakers, because of their long abolitionist tradition.

Furthermore, the Quakers had a long abolitionist tradition. The first antislavery document in American history had been drafted in 1688 by a group of Philadelphia Friends, and largely Quaker Pennsylvania had been among the first of the states to abolish slavery. Benjamin Lundy, who worked on the *Genius* with Garrison, was a Quaker, and Garrison appreciated Lundy's quiet self-assurance and certainty that slavery was a great wrong. As a Friend, Lundy had been steeped in antislavery sentiment from an early age, unlike most non-Quakers in America. During his months with Lundy, Garrison absorbed some of this sentiment and established a philosophical foundation on which to build. "I feel that I owe everything, instrumentally and under God," Garrison wrote on the occasion of Lundy's death, "to Benjamin Lundy"—and, by extension, to the Society of Friends.[85]

The Declaration of Independence

Garrison's other important influence was, perhaps surprisingly, a political document. The *Liberator* either ignored or despised all political documents—the Constitution, the Kansas-Nebraska Act, the Fugitive Slave Law—except the Declaration of Independence. In the development of Garrison's philosophy, the Declaration was as vital as the Bible, and indeed the *Liberator* often referred to the two of them together. "We plant ourselves upon the truths of Divine Revelation [that is, the Bible] and the Declaration of Independence as upon the EVERLASTING ROCK," Garrison wrote.[86]

Garrison was drawn to the "solemn and heaven-attested Declaration" for several reasons.[87] For one thing, the Declaration was written in high-flown, idealistic language that appealed to Garrison. Unlike the Constitution, for instance, the Declaration did not concern itself with issues of representation and other legalistic details. Rather, the Declaration addressed basic, natural laws and the rights of all people.

Garrison did not deal especially well with practical details in his writing, and the big ideas of the Declaration suited his temperament perfectly. The Declaration begins by stating that there are "certain unalienable rights" given all men by "their Creator," and goes on to name three: "Life, Liberty, and the pursuit of Happiness."[88] This recognition of natural rights and a higher law intrigued Garrison and led to some of his most impassioned *Liberator* editorials. Gradualism, he wrote in 1832, was "a fatal departure from the high road of justice into the bogs of expediency."[89] Garrison's nearly constant rejection of compromise in favor of a higher standard of justice and rights came directly from the Declaration.

"All Men Are Created Equal"

Garrison particularly admired certain phrases in the Declaration. "I assert [the slaves'] inalienable right to liberty and the pursuit of happiness," he wrote in 1842, making it clear that he considered slaves among those covered by the document.[90] He also appreciated the document's insistence that all men are created equal. It is doubtful that many of those who signed the document actually considered black men to be the equals of whites, but Garrison persisted in taking the language literally. His great sin, he wrote sarcastically in 1835, was "preaching the abominable and dangerous doctrine that 'all men are created equal.'"[91] Indeed, in his hands the phrase became a weapon and a revolutionary tool.

A second influence in the Declaration lay in the section that stated:

> Whenever any Form of Government becomes destructive of these ends [that is, the goal of helping ensure its people life, liberty, and the pursuit of happiness], it is the Right of the People to alter or abolish it, and to institute new Government, laying its foundation on such principles and organizing its powers in such form, as to them shall seem most likely to effect their Safety and Happiness.[92]

In whose interest was slavery? Garrison asked again and again. Perhaps slavery was valuable for the slave owners, but it did not at all help bring about the slaves' "Safety and Happiness." If the current form of government, which supported slavery, did not tend to increase the quality of life for slaves, Garrison reasoned, then it needed to be abolished: the Declaration itself said so. During most of his career, Garrison urged radical changes in the government, and he did so secure in the knowledge that the Declaration, in his eyes, required exactly that.

Garrison also enjoyed battling Southern slaveholders who revered the Declaration. Just as slaveholders misinterpreted the Bible, in his opinion, so too did they miss the main point of the Declaration. "*Who*

Though it was a political document and he abhorred government in general, the Declaration of Independence was a huge influence on Garrison.

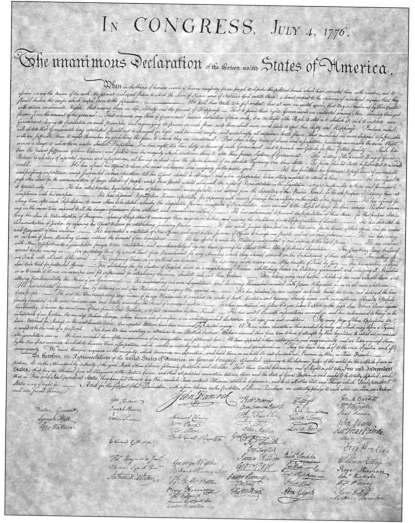

instigated John Brown?" he asked rhetorically after Brown's slave revolt failed and Southerners charged newspapers such as Garrison's with having egged him on. "It must have been Thomas Jefferson . . . who, as the author of the Declaration of Independence, proclaimed it to be a 'SELF-EVIDENT TRUTH, that all men are created equal, and endowed by their Creator with AN INALIENABLE RIGHT TO LIBERTY.'"[93] Such rebukes were commonplace in the *Liberator* when Garrison wrote about the hypocrisy of Southerners.

Hope

The Declaration, like the Bible, also provided hope for Garrison and his newspaper. Eventually, he was sure, the majority of the people would understand the connection between these two great works and the antislavery movement. They would see that the Declaration concerned not only white males but slaves and women as well; they would realize that Jesus was not interested in preserving the power of earthly governments, but focused on leading peaceful revolution that required overturning slavery.

In fact, despite its sarcasm, anger, and critical focus, the *Liberator* was fundamentally a hopeful document. "I feel as sure as that day will follow night," Garrison argued in 1839, "that the political action of this country will be purified and renovated," and that slavery would come to an end.[94] The Bible looked forward to the time when the kingdom of heaven would flourish on earth, a time perhaps distant but inevitable. As for the Declaration, its principles were clear, inspired, and rock solid. "As long as there remains a single copy of the Declaration of Independence, or of the Bible, in our land," Garrison wrote once, "we shall not despair."[95]

Limited Influence

Though the *Liberator* was influenced by many different sources, Garrison did not draw from those sources exactly what others saw in them. Garrison's vision was essentially individual. Enthusiastic as he was about Quakerism, for example, he never actually became a Quaker. Nor did the *Liberator* consistently reflect the nonviolence-at-any-cost attitude of many Friends, such as Benjamin Lundy. Thus, while the newspaper preached a Quaker-influenced philosophy, it stopped short of becoming a fully Quaker publication.

Similarly, Garrison often did not bring influences to their logical conclusions. His rejection of government, for instance, was certainly influenced by both the Bible and the Declaration of Independence. However, Garrison did not simply accept everything that these two documents had to say about the subject. The Declaration, after all,

Garrison and the Constitution

One document that was decidedly not a positive influence on the *Liberator* was the U.S. Constitution. Garrison distrusted, even hated, the Constitution. He saw it as a political document, first and foremost: not based on great sweeping principles like the Declaration of Independence, but rather a compromise born of expedience.

Worse, he saw the Constitution as a pro-slavery document. It embedded the idea of slavery into the founding of the nation, thus making it quite hard to dislodge and contaminating—in Garrison's eyes—the course of American history. He roared his disapproval whenever anyone tried to defend the Constitution on other grounds, or to argue that the Constitution could be interpreted as an antislavery document. His views are especially well described in this 1844 excerpt from the *Liberator*, quoted in Truman Nelson's *Documents of Upheaval*:

> It is absurd, it is false, it is an insult to the common sense of mankind, to pretend that the Constitution was intended to embrace the entire population of the country [that is, both whites and blacks] under its sheltering wings; or that the parties to it were actuated by a sense of justice and the spirit of impartial liberty; or that it needs no alteration, but only a new interpretation, to make it harmonize with the object aimed at by its adoption. . . . The truth is, our fathers were intent on securing liberty to *themselves*. . . . [T]hough *in words* they recognized occasionally the brotherhood of the human race, *in practice* they continually denied it.

In Garrison's view, the Constitution was an irreparably evil document: it allowed slavery, it was used by Southerners to justify slavery, and it represented the worst kind of compromising of ideals for political reasons. The *Liberator* regularly criticized it. Finally, Garrison burned a copy of the Constitution during a public meeting, with the typically Garrisonian words—as quoted in Louis Filler's *The Crusade Against Slavery*—"So perish all compromises with tyranny!"

OBSERVATIONS

On the Inflaving, importing and purchasing of

Negroes;

With some Advice thereon, extracted from the Epistle of the Yearly-Meeting of the People called QUAKERS, held at London in the Year 1748.

Anthony Benezet

When ye spread forth your Hands, I will hide mine Eyes from you, yea when ye make many Prayers I will not hear; your Hands are full of Blood. Wash ye, make you clean, put away the Evil of your Doings from before mine Eyes. Isa. 1, 15.

Is not this the Fast that I have chosen, to loose the Bands of Wickedness, to undo the heavy Burden, to let the Oppressed go free, and that ye break every Yoke, Chap. 58, 7.

Second Edition.

GERMANTOWN:
Printed by CHRISTOPHER SOWER. 1760.

The title page of the Book of Slavery.

did not condemn the use of force to change governments—indeed, it sparked a long and bloody war—yet Garrison rejected violence until quite late in his editorial career.

Likewise, Garrison's view of Jesus suggested that worldly governments were not a valid solution for worldly problems, yet Garrison advocated political disunion from the Southern states on many occasions. In the same way, Garrison used extremely violent language for a self-described Christian pacifist. And many Christian theologians would not interpret Jesus' life in such simple, unambiguous terms as did Garrison. This is not to say that Garrison's thinking was wrong or contradictory, but it does reveal Garrison's willingness to interpret the words of a source in the way that suited him.

Sometimes, too, Garrison simply ignored the full implications of a source. This is most obviously true in the case of the Bible, where the *Liberator* passed over or dismissed much of the Old Testament in its zeal to prove slavery a great wrong. He also ignored several New Testament passages that tended to support slavery. Garrison was not at all troubled by biblical verses that urged Christians to attend church services or that promoted the subservience of women. He had an ability to ignore what he disliked and nevertheless write as though the Bible were entirely in his favor.

Finally, Garrison's emphases could be misplaced. In "Casabianca," Felicia Hemans was most probably playing up the virtues of conventional morality—not a favorite theme of Garrison's—instead of encouraging readers to look for higher moral laws. The Bible was not primarily an antislavery document, no matter how Garrison chose to interpret it. Nor was the Declaration of Independence drafted to give African Americans equal rights with American whites.

Again, however, these different interpretations bothered Garrison not a bit. Throughout his career Garrison was more interested in advocacy than in coherent philosophy. While other reformers worried about consistency, Garrison fretted over results. And late in the 1850s, he even began to alter some of his most deeply held ideals in order to hasten the end of slavery. At heart, the *Liberator's* philosophy was not based on the Declaration of Independence, nor even on the New Testament. It was instead based on a single principle: Whatever will advance the cause of freeing the slaves is good, and should be supported. The newspaper's every word flowed directly from that precept.

CHAPTER 4 Reaction

The *Liberator* was not the only antislavery voice of its time. Several other newspapers, such as that of Illinois editor Elijah Lovejoy, devoted all or some of their content to abolition. Many Quakers, including Benjamin Lundy and feminist leader Lucretia Mott, spent much of their lives quietly working against slavery. Prudence Crandall tried to open a school for black girls; Lydia Maria Child wrote books refuting slaveholders' arguments point by point. A revivalist Protestant preacher named Theodore Weld gave speech after speech against slavery, detailing the horrors of the slave system until his voice literally gave out. Former slave Frederick Douglass was a strong and articulate spokesman for the abolition cause. Others, such as Southerner Levi Coffin, worked to help slaves escape to freedom.

Each of these antislavery leaders had a distinctive style and individual strengths. Each had clear successes in getting his or her message across, and obvious failures as well. To some audiences, Douglass's first-person account of life as a slave was most effective. To others, Weld's carefully researched recitation of the brutalities committed upon Southern slaves worked best. Those who planned escape routes and set up safe houses for runaway slaves changed fewer minds, but directly helped more slaves. In the same way, Garrison's often bitter arguments for immediate, nonpolitical

Quaker feminist Lucretia Mott devoted her entire life to ending slavery.

abolition struck a chord with some readers, though certainly not all.

Abolitionists' various styles did have one thing in common. Every antislavery activist met with widespread opposition from the South—and opposition from the North as well. In this realm, the *Liberator* headed the list. A barrage of protest, from angry rebuttals to threats, met Garrison's newspaper at every turn, a firestorm of controversy that went far beyond the *Liberator*'s limited circulation. A few abolitionists, like John Brown and Lovejoy, died for their cause, and Weld, among others, was reviled as much as Garrison. Nevertheless, what sets the *Liberator* apart from many of its counterparts is the strength and degree of the reaction against it.

Southerners

By all rights, the *Liberator* should never have come to the attention of most Southerners. As a struggling newspaper barely able to pay its own bills, far outshadowed by other prominent Boston periodicals, copies of the *Liberator* rarely reached beyond Philadelphia. However, a few early issues did make their way into Virginia and points south. The Southerners who read them mostly ignored Garrison's words, but some responded with anger equaling the newspaper's. "Your paper cannot be much longer tolerated," one Southerner warned him in a letter.[96]

To Garrison, of course, anger from the South was exactly what he desired. He wanted to annoy and irritate. Negative attention, to him, was far better than a complete lack of attention; with negative attention there would be controversy, dialogue, and above all *notice*. Garrison could not abide being ignored. Nor,

A white man takes aim on a runaway slave trying to swim for his freedom.

as it happened, could he deal with being merely one voice in a chorus. He had to stand out, and he did it through his use of intemperate, hostile language whenever possible.

A cycle began. Garrison reprinted Southerners' letters, the angrier the better, for all the world to see. He would then add, in inflammatory language, his commentary explaining why the correspondent's ideas were wrong, even evil. Before long Southern newspapers would reprint the original letters and Garrison's responses to them. These papers, in turn, would add their own commentary. Gradually, the debate moved across the South from paper to paper, and the name of the *Liberator* became known from Maryland to Texas. Garrison duly reported what these Southern editors said about him, and the cycle continued.

The death of slave revolt leader Nat Turner is depicted at the end of a white man's gun.

Nat Turner

The fledgling *Liberator* was only a minor irritant until August 1831. That month marked Nat Turner's rebellion. Turner, a slave and preacher from Southampton, Virginia, led a night attack on several plantations. About sixty whites were murdered before the rebellion was put down. Turner escaped into the swamps for several weeks; once captured, he was tried, convicted, and executed, along with his followers. In revenge for Turner's actions, white officials and marauders killed dozens of other blacks, most of whom knew nothing of Turner's plans.

Slave revolts in the South were actually very unusual. Turner's was the first organized attempt to kill whites in many years. However, slaveholders lived in fear of such rebellions. Blacks outnumbered whites in dozens of Southern counties; in places like coastal South Carolina, Tidewater Virginia, and the Mississippi Delta, whites were only a tiny minority. Given this imbalance and the brutality with which slaves often were treated, slave revolts were always a possibility. Even before Turner, few slaveholders went to bed at night absolutely certain that their slaves would not kill them as they slept. Slave owner Mary Chesnut, for instance, wrote of wondering how long it would be before all her slaves obeyed "the seductive and irresistible call: Rise, kill, and be free."[97]

Turner's rebellion, therefore, panicked Southerners. The unthinkable had happened and, across the region, slaveholders worried that their plantations would be next. Unwilling to attribute the rebellion to their poor treatment of slaves and slavery itself, the slaveholders looked for scapegoats. The answer, for many, was clear. The culprits were the abolitionists, who had been encouraging the slaves to revolt for quite some time. The governor of Virginia expressed the opinion of many when he wrote that the rebellion did not originate with Turner, but rather was "undoubtedly designed and matured by unrestrained fanatics in some of the neighboring states."[98]

And chief among these "unrestrained fanatics" was the angriest of all antislavery newspapers, the *Liberator*. To Southerners, it made perfect sense that the *Liberator* was behind the revolt. After all, it insulted the South at every turn, demanded immediate abolition in hateful, caustic terms, and reprinted Southern viewpoints only to mock them. A North Carolina newspaper minced no words. Turner, it wrote, was influenced by "an incendiary paper, the *Liberator*, published in either Boston or Philadelphia by a white man, with the avowed purpose of exciting rebellion in the South."[99]

"The Instigator of Human Butchery"

All at once the little Massachusetts newspaper took on a significance far beyond its size and means. Southern editors slammed Garrison, often—as the North Carolina report indicates—without knowing anything about him or having actually read any of his words. The *Liberator* became the definition of evil across the entire South. A Washington editor called Garrison "the instigator of human butchery . . . a deluded fanatic [and] a cut throat." As for the *Liberator* itself, it was "a diabolical paper, intended by its author to lead to precisely such results as the Southampton Tragedy."[100]

Garrison protested that his paper had no such intention. On one level he was quite right. In 1831, and indeed for many years afterward, he wrote clearly and strongly against slave uprisings. "We are horror-struck at the late tidings [news]," the *Liberator* editorialized upon learning of the revolt.[101] Besides, Turner's account indicated without a doubt that he had acted on his own. There was absolutely no evidence that Turner had ever heard of Garrison or seen a copy of the *Liberator*.

However, the Southerners who attacked him did have a point. Even while condemning those who rebelled, Garrison indirectly encouraged revolt. Again and again he stated that slaves would be justified should they choose to rise up against their brutal masters. Moreover, Garrison was delighted at the attention he was receiving and resolved to keep the issue alive. Instead of keeping silent on the subject of Turner's rebellion, he hammered away at the inevitability of future revolts if the South did not mend its ways. "If we would not see our land deluged in blood," he warned, "we must instantly burst the shackles of slaves."[102]

Partly as a result of Garrison's response, the South's attacks on the *Liberator* grew stronger. A section of the District of Columbia made it illegal for slaves or free blacks to read Garrison's newspaper. South Carolina banned the *Liberator* altogether and offered a reward of $1,500 for turning in anyone who broke the law. (Garrison joked that he was worth more than that.) Several cities and towns indicted Garrison for disturbing the peace. The state of Georgia went further:

> Resolved . . . that the sum of FIVE THOUSAND DOL-
> LARS, be . . . paid to any person or persons who shall arrest,
> bring to trial and prosecute to conviction under the laws of

Copies of the Liberator *are burned in Charleston, South Carolina, in response to Garrison's opinion that slaves would be justified in killing their masters.*

this State; the editor or publisher of a certain paper called the *Liberator*, published in the town of Boston.[103]

The war of words over Nat Turner eventually died down, but Southern hostility toward the *Liberator* did not. For the next thirty years, the *Liberator* was routinely attacked by Southern leaders and editors. In 1836 several states demanded that the North forbid newspapers such as the *Liberator* from discussing slavery in such angry terms. A Richmond newspaper threatened, "Let the hell-hounds of the North beware," in clear reference to Garrison.[104] In Charleston, South Carolina, Garrison was burned in effigy: that is, a figure representing him was set afire while a crowd watched and cheered. "The *Liberator* was made famous not by its Northern supporters," one historian concluded, "but by its Southern enemies."[105]

The North

The North, however, was scarcely more hospitable to Garrison's messages than was the South. For economic, political, and racial reasons many Northerners did not support abolition to any degree. Nor did many Northerners appreciate Garrison's other messages: against organized religion, for pacifism, against government. His ideas were too radical for most Northerners. "Abolitionist ravings," scoffed one Northern newspaper. A handbill posted in Boston accused him of "slandering Americans to the utmost of his power."[106] Rocks, eggs, and bricks were thrown at Garrison as he walked along the streets of Boston. He received death threats, too, and opponents erected a gallows outside his house.

Through much of the early 1830s, in fact, abolition—especially the extreme abolition advocated by the *Liberator*—was not a popular subject in Boston. Garrison had always had trouble finding places to give speeches. Nearly all influential city churches were closed to him, and so were many public buildings. Increasingly it seemed to Garrison that discussion of slavery was being gradually squeezed out, even in the supposedly tolerant North. Crowds cheered the mayor of Boston when he urged the North to accept "the South's claim to consider their slaves as cyphers or nonentities."[107] Moreover, he continued, Garrison's version of abolition was "not only imminently dangerous, but hostile to the spirit and the letter of the Constitution."[108] The *Liberator* bemoaned both the lack of empathy for slaves and the hostility toward free speech, but Garrison persisted.

Boston was not the only place where anti-abolition sentiment was strong. "Ohio will give no countenance to the followers of Garrison and [abolitionist Arthur] Tappan," a Cincinnati newspaper editorialized.[109]

William Lloyd Garrison trying to escape the mob.

New York City was worse. Garrison remembered arriving in New York to give a speech, only to be met by an angry mob urging him to go home. "As soon as I landed, I turned the city of New York upside down," he wrote. "Five thousand people turned out to see me tarred and feathered, but were disappointed."[110]

Matters came to a head in 1835, when Garrison gave a lecture to the Boston Female Antislavery Society. The combination of Garrison's inflammatory language, women's involvement in politics, and the *Liberator*'s constant agitation for the rights of blacks sparked the gathering of an angry mob outside the doors of the building where the meeting was held. The mob included, Garrison noted, not merely street toughs but also "gentlemen of property and standing"—the most respectable citizens of Boston.[111] They broke down the door and seized Garrison, crying, "We must have Garrison! Out with him! Lynch him!"[112] Garrison narrowly escaped harm, but was jailed for his own protection, and left the city the next day.

The *Liberator*'s response to this mob was predictable. "Charleston and New-Orleans have never acted so brutally," Garrison editorialized in the next issue of the paper. "Courageous cravens!"[113] Garrison reserved particular anger for the police and city government, which he charged had more or less ignored the mob. The police had allowed the crowd to destroy an antislavery placard, and, significantly, officers had made no effort to arrest the leaders of the mob.

Garrison also argued that virtually every newspaper in town ignored the violence, tacitly supporting it. In fact, at least one local paper had blamed Garrison and the rest of the abolitionists for the incident; Garrison, it wrote, was a "public agitator."[114] In any case, Garrison had been lucky to escape. The mob had demonstrated for all to see that many Northerners did take violent issue with what the *Liberator* said.

Other Abolitionists

But not everyone who disapproved of the *Liberator* was a vicious racist who hated the notion of emancipation. Among Garrison's harshest critics were his fellow abolitionists. Some of these men and women had legitimate differences of opinion with the *Liberator* on slavery and other issues. Others resented the attention Garrison was drawing. And still others feared that Garrison's extreme views were making the South dig in its heels, thus delaying the ultimate end of slavery.

Gently at first, but more and more strongly as time went on, Northern abolitionists cautioned Garrison to calm down and modify his voice. "Noise and combination is not always power," a clergyman warned.[115] Francis Wayland found the *Liberator*'s language "menacing and vindictive" and suggested that it would simply serve to harden the South against antislavery pleas from the North.[116] Garrison's support of side issues also troubled abolitionists. Garrison, wrote one, was intent on "making abolitionism a stalking-horse for no-governmentism, no-churchism, and every other insane whim."[117]

By 1840 many abolitionists were aligned solidly against Garrison. Colonization supporters were tired of being called "steeped in sin [and] deep in pollution."[118] Gradualists had written the *Liberator* off

A cartoon depicting an abolitionist meeting with Garrison.

long before; they did not appreciate the charge that they were somehow soft on slavery. Lyman Beecher took particular offense at Garrison's jibe that, for the first time in his ministerial career, he was recommending a "gradual abolition of wickedness."[119] Antislavery leaders who did not believe in nonviolence stood in opposition to the *Liberator*. So did those who looked for political solutions. Tensions were high on both sides: "I hate them with a perfect hatred," wrote a minister about Garrison and those who agreed with him.[120]

Certainly, the abolitionists' negative reaction was in part a response to Garrison's own intolerance. The *Liberator* lashed out at friend as well as at enemy. At times it seemed as if no one was pure enough for Garrison. "Blind leaders of the blind, dumb dogs that cannot bark," he called a group of gradualist ministers.[121] Garrison broke with Frederick Douglass over several issues, including Douglass's interest in exploring political solutions for slavery. He criticized Harriet Beecher Stowe, the author of the antislavery novel *Uncle Tom's Cabin*, for racist depictions of slaves. At various times the *Liberator* took on other antislavery activists, too, including Arthur Tappan, Abby Kelley Foster, and Wendell Phillips, all at one time or another allies of Garrison's.

Typically, Garrison accepted no blame whatsoever for these rifts. Every argument was someone else's fault: They supported the wrong position, they were moving in the wrong direction, or they were not moving quickly enough in the right direction. The right direction and the right position, always, were Garrison's. "Let the blame rest on the heads of those who have virtually abandoned our cause," he wrote to a friend, "if they ever belonged to it."[122] It never occurred to him that others might be doing good work, too, although in a somewhat different way. In general, Garrison had extreme difficulty admitting that he was wrong, and he rarely did so—a trait that no doubt added to the negative reaction he so often received even from fellow abolitionists.

Garrison criticized Harriet Beecher Stowe for her racist depiction of slavery.

Friends

Nevertheless, the *Liberator* did have its friends. The staunchest among them, as mentioned, were Northern blacks. The first issue of the *Liberator* was made possible in part by a large group of Philadel-

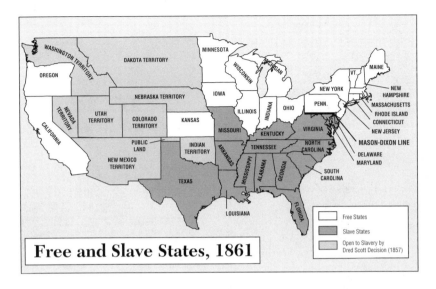

Free and Slave States, 1861

Free States
Slave States
Open to Slavery by
Dred Scott Decision (1857)

new parts of the nation, where neither North nor South exercised sole jurisdiction. Thus, they urged that the new residents of a territory be allowed to decide the slavery question for themselves.

Most Northerners, however, were not pleased with this suggestion. They did not like Southerners changing the rules and wiping out years of carefully controlled compromise. They also began to wonder how far the South would go. If laws could be changed so that slavery was legal in Nebraska, some asked, why would the South stop there? Perhaps radical Southerners would try next to foist slavery back on Pennsylvania or into Illinois. By 1848, the concern was great enough to bring about the formation of a new political party, the Free Soilers. "We inscribe on our banner 'Free Soil, Free Speech, Free Labor, and Free Men,'" the party's slogan read, "and under it will fight on . . . until a triumphant victory shall reward our exertions."[126]

Garrison, among others, thundered his disapproval of the Southern strategy. He poured particular venom on the 1854 Kansas-Nebraska Act, which among other things potentially opened the previously free territory of Nebraska to slavery. Garrison objected to the new policy partly because any extension of slavery threatened the cause of abolition. But Garrison's fury also had another cause. The South, by demanding the opening of new territories to slavery, was trying to run the whole country. As Garrison put it in a New York City speech later reprinted in the *Liberator*, the South was attempting to make the North "cower and obey like a plantation slave."[127]

There was an interesting footnote to this speech. Four years earlier, Garrison had been in New York City, then a stronghold of anti-abolitionist sentiment, and had given a lecture to a crowd of local whites. His earlier speech had been booed; hecklers shouted insults at him and tried to disrupt the proceedings at every turn. But in 1854 he received cheers and applause from another largely white group for his words. Ordinary New Yorkers agreed that the South was demanding too much. For the first time in the *Liberator*'s existence, its words and accusations were striking a popular chord.

Fugitive Slaves

But expansion of slavery was not the only issue tending to drive the two regions apart. The Fugitive Slave Law, a part of the Compromise of 1850, was another. The Fugitive Slave Law affirmed that slavemasters had absolute rights to their runaway slaves, no matter where the slaves now lived or how long they had been gone. The South believed that this was a sensible and just law. If a cow wandered away from a farm, the owner would expect a

CAUTION!!
COLORED PEOPLE
OF BOSTON, ONE & ALL,
You are hereby respectfully CAUTIONED and advised, to avoid conversing with the
Watchmen and Police Officers of Boston,
For since the recent ORDER OF THE MAYOR & ALDERMEN, they are empowered to act as
KIDNAPPERS
AND
Slave Catchers,
And they have already been actually employed in KIDNAPPING, CATCHING, AND KEEPING SLAVES. Therefore, if you value your LIBERTY, and the *Welfare of the Fugitives* among you, *Shun* them in every possible manner, as so many *HOUNDS* on the track of the most unfortunate of your race.
Keep a Sharp Look Out for KIDNAPPERS, and have TOP EYE open.
APRIL 24, 1851.

A poster warning fugitive slaves in the Boston area to steer clear of police officers.

neighbor to return it. Similarly, stolen tools or horses still belonged, by law, to their original owners. The same, Southerners reasoned, ought to be true with slaves as well. After all, slaves were property.

The North, however, disagreed. Having no stake in slavery, Northerners tended to believe that a slave who managed to run away ought to be applauded, not arrested. Once again, too, the law appeared to be the pet project of the South, not a law that benefited everybody. Many Northerners objected to a system that called on them to return these slaves to their masters, and which permitted masters—or their agents— to come North to search for their runaways. "No slave-hunt in our borders," wrote poet John Greenleaf Whittier, "no pirate on our strand!"[128]

Again, Garrison weighed in on the controversy. He filled the *Liberator* with protests of the law, both his own and those written by others, and he urged that the law not be followed. At a Fourth of July celebration in 1854, he burned a copy of the Fugitive Slave Law, intoning, "And let all the people say, 'Amen.'"[129] Deep down, however, Garrison liked the law, not because of its immediate goals, which of course he hated, but because he believed it would show Northerners the true horrors of slavery.

He was right. Just as had happened with the question of slavery in the territories, the Fugitive Slave Law sparked opposition among many who did not necessarily call themselves abolitionists. A resident of one Michigan county noted that his fellow citizens had not cared much one way or the other about slavery until the passage of the new law. "It has greatly changed since," he added shortly afterward. "Our citizens side almost with entire unanimity with the poor captives and fugitives, and there is deep feeling on the subject."[130] Many Northern states, cities, and counties passed laws to make it more difficult to take fugitive slaves back. In some places, including Boston, antislavery mobs surrounded fugitives who were in danger and spirited them away to safety.

All this, of course, annoyed the South, which fought back. President Millard Fillmore issued a proclamation in 1851 decrying the "scandalous outrages" committed by a group of Bostonians who rescued a fugitive and "calling on all well-disposed citizens to rally to the support of the laws of their country."[131] Southerners could not understand why the North refused to support a fugitive slave law. In their estimation, it could only mean that the North was less than fully committed to the South's right to allow slavery at all. And so the two sides drifted further apart, mutually suspicious and growing steadily more so.

The *Liberator*'s Role

It would be wrong to say that the abolitionists caused the growing split between North and South, but there is no doubt that they played a significant role. To Southerners of the 1850s, the existence of publications like the *Liberator* was proof that Northerners were out to destroy their way of life. The fact that Northern governments refused to shut the offending papers down, or silence the abolitionists by throwing

A runaway slave makes his way toward freedom.

them in jail, infuriated the South, too. Worse, it strengthened Southern feelings that the North had a secret agenda: trying to force the South to give up its slaves.

In turn, the louder the South complained, the more Northerners began to dig in their heels. They believed that the South was overly sensitive and trying too hard to defend its institution, but mostly they resented the South's attempt to set national policy around only one issue. That one issue, slavery, was not even important to most Northerners, but the South seemed not to want to be convinced. Disgusted, Northerners began to view everything the South asked for with suspicion. The overall effect was to make each side wonder whether continued political union was in anyone's best interest. As one of the most obnoxious of all the abolitionists, Garrison was among the main causes of this split.

The *Liberator* played another role, too. Not only did it bait the South, but it also set an example for the North. True, the example was often hard to find beneath all the poisonous insults Garrison delivered to his enemies, and it is doubtful that reading an issue of the *Liberator* convinced many wavering Northerners to support the antislavery side of the debate. Nevertheless, the *Liberator's* constant emphasis on moral force had value. Its idealism, its certainty that slavery was wrong, its unwillingness to yield even the most trivial points all combined to make Garrison's newspaper a beacon of light for the more radical abolitionists. They persevered, in part, because Garrison did; they could continue to work in the face of opposition, in part, because Garrison could; they had the utmost faith in the rightness of their cause, in part, because Garrison had. Even abolitionists with whom he disagreed drew inspiration from the *Liberator*.

Yet moral force did not, by itself, end slavery; it took a war to do that. On the surface, fighting a war—even a war against slavery— might seem very much a contradiction of Garrison's principles. The *Liberator* had so often editorialized against violent solutions. Moreover, disunion was a political move, again not something that Garrison typically defended. However, even the war did bear the marks of Garrison's influence. For by the middle 1850s, the *Liberator* had made two major changes in philosophy.

Even after the Emancipation Proclamation, relationships between blacks and whites were still unequal.

Pacifism

The first major philosophical change the newspaper underwent involved pacifism. Garrison's devotion to nonviolence had always seemed somewhat suspect. Even while decrying slave revolts, he often appeared to be encouraging or at least justifying them. By the late 1850s, that contradiction was more and more obvious. He gave the usual censure to John Brown's raid, but added that it was not a violation of his principles to "wish success to any slave insurrection in the South."[132] For a self-described pacifist to wish success to violent slave revolt certainly indicated a change in Garrison's thinking.

The 1854 Republican Party building in Ripon, Wisconsin.

Garrison defended his change of heart on two levels. Slavery was such a persistent evil, Garrison decided, that it was no longer appropriate to ask slaves to simply turn the other cheek. Slaves had tried that for two hundred years, and slavery had become more, not less, entrenched. Perhaps it was time to try a new tack.

Moreover, there was a fundamental problem with nonresistance, Garrison decided. Nonresistance ought to mean no weapons for *anyone*. However, all the pacifism in the world had not kept weapons out of the hands of the slaveholders. "I . . . disarm John Brown," he announced, "and every slave at the South. But I do not stop there. . . . I also disarm, in the name of God, every slaveholder and tyrant in the world."[133] Unfortunately, nonresistance did not seem likely to reach the ears of the armed South any time soon, another reason why Garrison gradually relaxed his doctrine.

Politics

At the same time, the *Liberator* began to take government much more seriously as a possible solution to slavery. Garrison had taken a surprisingly benign view of the Free Soil Party in 1848. He believed it was a hopelessly political organization that could never represent "true abolitionism."[134] He saw it as fundamentally racist, too, which it was. Moreover, Garrison was not drawn to the party's focus on the spread of slavery; he preferred to attack it where it already existed and could not understand why the Free Soilers did not share his attitude. However, the *Liberator* did give the party's candidates and platform a certain amount of encouragement, and Garrison admitted that the Free Soil movement represented at least "a token of progress."[135]

Free Soilers
and Republicans

The terms *antislavery* and *abolition*
seem more or less interchangeable today,
but they were not so during the 1840s and
1850s. Abolitionists were those who worked for
the end to slavery altogether, whether gradually or immediately. Although the Free Soilers and the Republicans
have both been described as abolitionist in character, that word
is not strictly accurate.

Neither the Republicans nor the Free Soilers were interested in
destroying slavery where it already existed (although each had activists
who were). Instead, the goal of both was to keep slavery out of the
western territories. Thus, they called themselves antislavery, not abolitionist. They stood in opposition to the expansion of slavery into
areas where it did not exist, and they were far from willing to help support slavery in the South, but they made it quite clear that they were
not interested in attacking slavery where it was already entrenched.
While the *Liberator* applauded both groups' antislavery platforms,
Garrison continually urged them to become more abolitionist as well.

The *Liberator's* stance regarding the Free Soil movement, however, would surface again a few years later. In 1854 the Republican
Party was founded. Like the Free Soilers, its platform staunchly opposed any further expansion of slavery in the territories. At first Garrison treated the Republicans as he had treated the Free Soil
movement, but as they grew more and more powerful his position
began to change. For the first time there was a possibility that an
openly antislavery party might actually win something—as one historian put it, that the Republicans would be "history's vehicle, the train
that would at last pull the abolition car into the station."[136]

Thus, without actually joining the Republicans or endorsing their
ideas, Garrison began to throw grudging support to the new party. He
bitterly criticized the Republicans when they seemed to back away
from antislavery campaign promises, and he wished that they, too,
would be less racist and more abolition-minded. Still, his tone was
different, and the reason was clear: He now knew that it would take
a mixture of politics and moral force to bring slavery to an end.

The *Liberator* used the Republicans' rise, too, to try to mend the
breach between antislavery politicians and moral abolitionists. Garrison,
of course, was a moral abolitionist, but he now saw the need for com-
bining forces with the politicians and those who accepted governmental

solutions. This meeting of the minds would be not "*mere* Politics," Garrison hastened to add, but "a common gathering of the people of the North to effect a common deliverance."[137] Call it what he would, however, Garrison was, perhaps for the first time, recognizing the importance of political and governmental solutions in achieving his goal.

Thus, by 1861, William Lloyd Garrison found himself in a position he would probably have thought impossible just ten years before: in cautious support of the Civil War. The emphasis was still very much on the word "cautious." Garrison grew impatient with the slow pace of the war and condemned Lincoln's early unwillingness to say the battles were about freeing the slaves. He wrote often in the *Liberator* of his fears that the war would end with things going back to the way they were before, abandoning the slaves.

However, Garrison was also willing to give credit where credit was due. "When I remember how fearfully pro-slavery was the public sentiment of the North," he wrote in 1864, "when I remember what he has had to deal with . . . and then remember that Abraham Lincoln has struck the chains from the limbs of more than three millions of slaves . . . I do not feel disposed, for one, to take this occasion, or any occasion, to say anything very harshly against Abraham Lincoln."[138] The Civil War was at once a violent and a political solution, and Garrison, however grudgingly, supported it. That war, too, is therefore part of the *Liberator's* legacy.

A Task Completed

In 1865, the Civil War ended in defeat for the rebelling Confederacy. The victorious Union abolished slavery for good. What was left of the armies of both sides returned home. And William Lloyd Garrison, after nearly thirty-five years of uninterrupted publication of the *Liberator*, called it quits. The last issue of the newspaper rolled off Garrison's presses on December 29, 1865.

Garrison had started the newspaper to eradicate slavery, and now that task was finished. It seemed right, he said, to "let [the *Liberator's*] existence cover the historic period of the great struggle."[139] Moreover, Garrison was clearly weary of the battle. "Most happy am I to be no longer in conflict with the mass of my fellow-countrymen on the subject of slavery," he wrote in the final issue, demonstrating his willingness to put the slavery argument behind him.[140] It is hard to imagine Garrison ever wanting to be in harmony with the general public.

After closing the *Liberator*, Garrison went into semiretirement. He continued to be active politically for a number of years, most notably writing and lecturing about the unfair treatment of blacks during the postwar period known as Reconstruction. However, never

Lincoln and Moral Force

The Emancipation Proclamation, issued by Abraham Lincoln in 1862, took effect on January 1, 1863. Technically it did absolutely nothing for any slave. The document freed all slaves in areas held by the Confederate States—areas, obviously, out of the reach of the federal government. Slaves who lived in the loyal border states, such as Kentucky and Missouri, and in areas of the Confederacy under Union control, such as parts of Tennessee and Louisiana, were specifically excluded from the proclamation.

Nevertheless, the proclamation was joyful news for abolitionists. "THREE MILLIONS OF SLAVES SET FREE!" the *Liberator* headlined in bold type, as quoted in Mayer's *All on Fire: William Lloyd Garrison and the Abolition of Slavery*. "GLORY HALLELUJAH!" With the document, Lincoln had made it clear that this was to be a war on slavery. But the proclamation had done more. It had, as Mayer put it, "endowed the war with a fresh and hallowed purpose." Freeing the slaves was now the highly moral and just work of the U.S. Army.

For the first time an influential American politician had looked at slavery and found it wrong: not wrong-but-politically-acceptable, not wrong-but-not-evil-either, but rather plain and simply wrong. "Upon this act," Lincoln wrote, as quoted in Everett's *Slavery*, "sincerely believed to be an act of justice . . . I invoke the considerate judgment of mankind, and the gracious favor of Almighty God." Those words echoed the *Liberator* in content if not in style. The Emancipation Proclamation relied on moral force to make its point, and moral force was nothing if not a Garrisonian ideal.

President Abraham Lincoln signs the Emancipation Proclamation giving freedom to all blacks.

again did Garrison respond to any issue with the same vehemence, absorption, and interest that he had given to the fight against slavery. Superseded by younger, more active leaders, his name drifted out of public awareness. In declining health during his later years, he died in 1879 already considered a man who had done great things in his time, but relegated to the past.

Postwar Influence

The *Liberator*'s influence after the war is difficult to evaluate. A clear line runs from the words of the *Liberator* to the Civil War and the freeing of the slaves. Though other abolitionist voices, such as Weld's or Douglass's, may have been more palatable or more widely heard heard than Garrison's, and though the growing conflict between North and South was sparked by economic and social forces besides slavery, it is nevertheless easy to see the connection between the *Liberator*'s message and the end of slavery.

To a large degree, however, the influence of the *Liberator* stopped there. The war was over, the slaves were freed; Garrison went into a relatively quiet retirement. His words no longer seemed relevant. To be sure, Garrison expressed his opinions on Reconstruction and the role of blacks in a newly free society. In his eyes, the federal government needed to safeguard the rights of Southern blacks. He criticized policies that allowed blacks to be victimized by the white majority, or, as he put it, a policy that "sustains might against right . . . the rich and powerful against the poor and unprotected."[141] There were occasional flashes of his former rhetoric: Shortly before he died, Garrison condemned the "weak, timid, purblind compromising element in the Republican party."[142] But Garrison does not loom large in the history of Reconstruction.

Nor did Garrison continue his work in most other areas. Despite his courageous stand for women's rights before the Civil War, he seemed to backslide afterward. Asked by suffragist Susan B. Anthony to help circulate a women's rights petition to Congress, Garrison refused. "Even as a matter of agitation," he told her, "I do not think it would pay."[143] His support of the war had compromised his pacifism and made him less appealing to new leaders who adopted an antigovernment stance. In fact, reform movements in the United States seemed increasingly political- and civic-minded, and those who rejected politics in favor of moral persuasion rarely cited Garrison as an influence.

Gandhi and King

Likewise, the moral and political movements of the modern age can only be linked indirectly to Garrison. Several twentieth-century leaders, notably Mohandas Gandhi in India and Martin Luther King Jr. in the United States, have led social movements similar in philosophy—if not in tone—to Garrison's particular brand of abolitionism. Both preached a policy of nonviolence, and both King and Gandhi grounded their words and deeds in religion, just as Garrison did. Yet neither King nor Gandhi attributed much of their thinking to Garrison's influence. Gandhi never mentioned Garrison in his autobiography, and King's references to the *Liberator* are rare indeed. Their biographers, too, seldom if ever make note of Garrison or the *Liberator*.

Mohandas K. Gandhi has been compared to William Lloyd Garrison for standing up against injustice in the face of controversy.

Still, the connections are only obscured, not nonexistent. "[The *Liberator's*] devotion to nonresistance," writes a contemporary historian, "became a demonstration of soul-force, an embodiment of truthful witness that M.K. Gandhi would, a century later, describe as *satyagraha*."[144] Both Gandhi and Garrison intended their nonresistance to be active, not passive: Rather than simply giving in, each wanted to force society to examine itself critically and to confront the violence and evil that it allowed, even encouraged. Whether Gandhi knew it or not, he was restating ideas expressed a century before by Garrison.

Similarly, King drew much from the *Liberator*. King combined an unshakable faith in the future with a certainty that evil was afoot in the world. He was both an agitator and a dreamer, a man who could state clearly all that was wrong with American society and in the next breath describe his conception of what things would look like when his vision was realized. The same was true of Garrison. Few Americans combined these two qualities so well as these two men. For this, if for nothing else, their names deserve to be linked.

In fact, Gandhi and King drew more from Garrison than they knew; the similarities in thoughts and ideals were not mere coincidence. Garrison had always acted as an outsider. He reveled in "causes which, being righteous, are unpopular."[145] He was most comfortable in the role of gadfly, and his mockery of those who disagreed with him led many people to disassociate themselves from him. In the years up to and immediately following the Civil War, many people did just that—abolitionists stung by his criticism, pacifists who considered Garrison insufficiently radical, politicians who dismissed Garrison for his contempt of government.

Yet the *Liberator* did influence many of these Americans, whether they chose to admit it or not. And in a roundabout way, some of these influences have persisted into modern times. Frederick Douglass is one good example. Douglass has been cited as an inspiration by several generations of African Americans. Douglass's ideas, of course, came from many different places, and he synthesized them into something completely new, but much of Douglass's thinking was directly influenced by his old friend Garrison. Thus, those who attribute some of their philosophy to Douglass are following the lead set down by Garrison a century and a half ago.

The *Liberator*'s Legacy

Likewise, much of what the *Liberator* said was adopted by Massachusetts philosopher Henry David Thoreau. Thoreau, a contemporary of Garrison's and occasional contributor to the *Liberator*, is best known today as the author of *Walden* and "Civil Disobedience"; as an abolitionist and thinker, he was given to Garrison-sounding statements like "Any man more right than his neighbors constitutes a majority of one."[146] As did Douglass, Thoreau put his own spin on Garrison's ideas. He rejected some outright, took others further than Garrison had, and altered still others to suit himself. Nevertheless, Thoreau was influenced by the *Liberator*, and Thoreau, in turn, has been cited as a major influence by many later thinkers, including Gandhi, King, and the Russian writer Leo Tolstoy.

But perhaps the *Liberator*'s clearest legacy lies not in the Civil War, nor in the career of Martin Luther King, nor even in the freedom of 4 million slaves. Perhaps what most set the *Liberator* apart was Garrison's absolute determination to say what he thought, no matter the consequences. That courage and drive was commendable then, and is today. Wherever people find the courage to stand up for their beliefs, they are following the lead of the *Liberator*. Whenever people refuse to stop working for what they believe is right, even in the face of opposition, they are acting on Garrisonian principles. And all activists who struggle to make themselves heard take heart, whether they know it or not, in the example of Garrison and the *Liberator*. The *Liberator* showed that social activism can succeed against the odds, against those in authority, and above all against the evils of society. Perhaps that is the most important legacy of all.

Appendix

Selections from the *Liberator*, 1831–1865

Document 1: First issue, January 1, 1831

An excerpt from a poem written by Garrison, describing his anti-slavery yet pacifist philosophy in a nutshell.

> Not by the sword shall your deliverance be;
> Not by the shedding of your masters' blood;
> Not by rebellion, or foul treachery.
> Upswinging suddenly, like swelling flood:
> Revenge and rapine ne'er did bring forth good.
> God's time is best!—nor will it long delay:
> Even now your barren cause begins to bud,
> And glorious shall the fruit be!—Watch and pray,
> For, lo! the kindling dawn, that ushers in the day!
>
>   G——

Document 2: *Definitions, January 8, 1831*

In this excerpt, Garrison points out many of the inconsistencies and evils of pro-slavery rhetoric. His contrasting of the Southern perceptions of white people or animals versus Southern perceptions of black people is well-reasoned and a typical Garrisonian line of argument.

1. All men are born equal, and entitled to protection, excepting those whose skins are black and hair woolly; or, to prevent mistake, excepting Africans, and their descendants.

2. If white men are ignorant and depraved, they ought freely to receive the benefits of education; but if black men are in this condition, common sense dictates that they should be held in bondage, and never instructed.

3. He who steals a sheep, or buys one of a thief, deserves severe punishment. He who steals a negro, or buys him of a kidnapper, is blameless. Why? Because a sheep can be eaten, and a negro cannot; because *he* has a *black* fleece, and *it* a *white* one; (1) because the law asserts that this distinction is just—and law, we all know, is founded in equity; and because pure benevolence actuates in the one case, and downright villany [*sic*] in the other.

4. The color of the skin determines whether a man has a soul or not. If white, he has an immortal essence; if black, he is altogether beastly. Mulattoes, however, derive no benefit from this rule.

5. The blacks ought to be held in fetters, because they are too stupid to take care of themselves; at least, we are not so stupid as to suffer them to make the experiment.

6. To kidnap children on the coast of Africa is a horrid crime, deservedly punishable with death; but he who steals them, in this country, as soon as they are born, performs not merely an innocent but a praiseworthy act.

7. In Africa, a man who buys or sells another, is a monster of hell. In America, he is an heir of heaven.

8. A man has a right to heap unbounded execration upon the foreign slave trade, and the abettors thereof; but if he utter a sentiment derogatory to the domestic traffic, or to those who assist in the transportation of victims, he is to be imprisoned for publishing a libel, and sentenced to pay a fine of not less than one thousand dollars.

9. He who calls American slaveholders *tyrants*, is a fool, a fanatic, or a madman;

but if he apologise for monarchical governments, or an hereditary aristocracy, set him down as a tory, and a traitor to his country.

10.   There is not the least danger of a rebellion among the slaves; and even if they should revolt *en masse*, what could they do? Their united physical force would be utterly contemptible.

11.   None but fanatics or idiots desire immediate abolition. If the slaves were liberated at once, our throats would be cut, and our houses pillaged and burnt!

12.   Our slaves must be educated for freedom. Our slaves must never learn the alphabet, because knowledge would teach them to throw off their yoke.

13.   People at the north have no right to alleviate physical suffering, or illumine spiritual darkness, at the south; but they have a right to assist the Greeks, or the Hindoos, or any foreign nation.

14.   Were the slaves, goaded to desperation, to rise against their masters, the free states are constitutionally bound to cut their throats! "The receiver is as bad as the thief." The free states receive and consume the productions of slave labor! The District of Columbia is national property: slavery exists in that District! Yet the free states are not involved in the guilt of slavery!

15.   A white man, who kills a tyrant, is a hero, and deserves a monument. If a slave kill his master, he is a murderer, and deserves to be burnt.

16.   The slaves are kept in bondage *for their own good*. Liberty is a curse to the free people of color—their condition is worse than that of the slaves! Yet it would be very wicked to bind them with fetters for *their* good!

17.   The slaves are contented and happy. If sometimes they are so ungrateful or deluded as to abscond, it is pure philanthropy that induces their masters to offer a handsome reward for their detection.

18.   Blacks have no intellect. The laws, at the south, which forbid their instruction, were not enacted because it was supposed these brutes had brains, or for the sake of compliment, but are owing simply to an itch for superfluous legislation.

19.   Slaves are held as property. It is the acme of humanity and justice, therefore, in the laws, to recognise them also as moral agents, and punish them in the most aggravated manner, if they perpetrate a crime; though they cannot read, and have neither seen nor known the laws!

Document 3: "Your Rod of Oppression Be Broken," January 10, 1845

This excerpt is a good example of the violent imagery Garrison loved to use. It also demonstrates his desire to move away from political solutions—except, perhaps, disunion with the South—and toward moral persuasion instead.

Tyrants of the old world! contemners of the rights of man! disbelievers in human freedom and equality! enemies of mankind! console not yourselves with the delusion, that REPUBLICANISM and the AMERICAN UNION are synonymous terms—or that the downfall of the latter will be the extinction of the former, and, consequently, a proof of the incapacity of the people for self-government, and a confirmation of your own despotic claims! Your thrones must crumble to dust; your sceptre of dominion drop from your powerless hands; your rod of oppression be broken; yourselves so vilely abased, that there shall be "none so poor to do you reverence." The will of God, the beneficent Creator of the human family, cannot always be frustrated. It is his will that every form of usurpation, every kind of injustice, every device of tyranny, shall come to nought; that peace, and liberty, and righteousness, shall "reign from sea to sea, and from the rivers to the ends of the earth"; and that, throughout the earth, in the fulness of a sure redemption, there shall be "none to molest or make afraid." Humanity, covered with gore, cries with a voice that pierces the heavens. "HIS WILL BE DONE!" Justice, discrowned by the hand of violence, exclaims in tones of deep solemnity, "HIS WILL BE DONE!" Liberty, burdened with chains, and driven into exile, in thunder-tones responds, "HIS WILL BE DONE!"

Tyrants! know that the rights of man are inherent and unalienable, and therefore, not to be forfeited by the failure of any form of government, however democratic. Let the American Union perish; let these allied States be torn with faction, or drenched in blood; let this republic realize the fate of Rome and Carthage, of Babylon and Tyre; still those rights would remain undiminished in strength, unsullied in purity, unaffected in value, and sacred as their Divine Author. If nations perish, it is not because of their devotion to liberty, but for their disregard of its requirements. Man is superior to all political compacts, all governmental arrangements, all religious institutions. As means to an end, these may sometimes be useful, though never indispensable; but that end must always be the freedom and happiness of man, INDIVIDUAL MAN. It can never be true that the public good requires the violent sacrifice of any, even the humblest citizen; for it is absolutely dependent on his preservation, not destruction. To do evil that good may come, is equally absurd and criminal. The time for the overthrow of any government, the abandonment of any alliance, the subversion of any institution, is, whenever it justifies the immolation of the individual to secure the general welfare; for the welfare of the many cannot be hostile to the safety of the few. In all agreements, in all measures, in all political or religious enterprises, in all attempts to redeem the human race, man, as an individual, is to be held paramount:—

"Him first, him last, him midst, and without end."

Document 4: *"John Brown Was Right,"* September 7, 1860.

This excerpt makes clear some of Garrison's reasoning about morality. If Washington was right to fight against tyrants, even to the death, then so too was John Brown.

. . .*John Brown was right*, because he faithfully 'remembered those in bonds as bound with them,' and did for them what he would have had them do for him in like circumstances.

John Brown was right, because he abhorred the practice of reducing to chains and slavery those whom God created 'but a little lower than the angels.'

John Brown was right, because he denied the validity of unrighteous and tyrannical enactments, and maintained the supremacy and binding obligation of the 'Higher Law.'

John Brown was right in all that he did—in his spirit and object, in his measures and warlike instruments, in taking the Arsenal and capturing Col. Washington, in killing 'Mr. Beckham, the Mayor, and Mr. Boerly, the grocer'—if Washington and Hancock and Warren were right—if Putnam, and Prescott, and the soldiers under them, on Bunker Hill, were right—if the Revolutionary struggle was right—if Wallace, and Tell, and Wrinkelreid, and Leonidas were right, in resisting tyranny unto blood! Only John Brown was before them all, and nobler than any of them, inasmuch as he gave his life to free others of a different race from a horrible bondage, with a spirit more than patriotic, because deeply religious and profoundly reverent toward God.

The *Courier* is politically foolish and morally demented in supposing that any party capital is to be made in the old Bay State, or out of it, in stabbing the memory and insulting the grave of John Brown, whom Christendom has already apotheosised as one of the bravest and noblest of those who have fallen martyrs to a great idea. It may rant and rave, give its sympathies to the traffickers in human flesh, and advocate the right to hunt slaves on Massachusetts soil, but it cannot stop the march of Freedom.

Document 5: *"Slaveholding is a Crime,"* June 28, 1839

Garrison here explains that the moral must precede the political in abolition. Slavery, after all, he says, is a moral crime, not so much a legal one.

Once more, I beg not to be misapprehended. I have always expected, I still expect, to see abolition at the ballot-box, renovating the political action of the country—dispelling the sorcery influences of party—breaking asunder the fetters of political servitude—stirring up the torpid consciences of voters—substituting anti-slavery for pro-slavery representatives in every legislative assembly—modifying and rescinding all laws which sanction slavery. But this political reformation is to be effected solely by a change in the moral vision of the people—not by attempting to prove that it is the duty of every abolitionist to be a voter, but that it is the duty of every voter to be an abolitionist. By converting electors to the doctrine that slavery ought to be immediately abolished, a rectified political action is the natural consequence; for where this doctrine is received into the soul, the soul-carrier may be trusted any where, that he will not betray the cause of bleeding humanity. As to the height and depth, the length and breadth of CHRISTIANITY, it is not the province of abolition to decide; but only to settle one point—to wit, that slaveholding is a crime under all circumstances, leaving those who believe in the doctrine to carry out their principles, with all fidelity, in whatever sphere they may be called upon to act, but not authoritatively determining whether they are bound to be members of the church, or voters at the polls. It has never been a difficult matter to induce men to go to the ballot-box; but the grand difficulty ever has been, and still is, to persuade them to carry a good conscience thither, and act as free moral agents, not as the tools of party.

Document 6: "To the Slaves," June 2, 1843

Here Garrison pledges his support to the slaves and reassures them that he, at least, will not forget their struggles. This excerpt is typical of many he ran over the years.

Take courage! Be filled with hope and comfort! Your redemption draws nigh, for the Lord is mightily at work in your behalf. Is it not frequently the darkest before daybreak? The word has gone forth that you shall be delivered from your chains, and it has not been spoken in vain.

Although you have many enemies, yet you have also many friends—warm, faithful, sympathizing, devoted friends—who will never abandon your cause; who are pledged to do all in their power to break your chains; who are laboring to effect your emancipation without delay, in a peaceable manner, without the shedding of blood; who regard you as brethren and countrymen, and fear not the frowns or threats of your masters. They call themselves abolitionists. They have already suffered much, in various parts of the country, for rebuking those who keep you in slavery—for demanding your immediate liberation—for revealing to the people the horrors of your situation—for boldly opposing a corrupt public sentiment, by which you are kept in the great southern prison-house of bondage. Some of them have been beaten with stripes; others have been stripped, and covered with tar and feathers; others have had their property taken from them, and burnt in the streets; others have had large rewards offered by your masters for their seizure; others have been cast into jails and penitentiaries; others have been mobbed and lynched with great violence; others have lost their reputation, and been ruined in their business; others have lost their lives. All these, and many other outrages of an equally grievous kind, they have suffered for your sakes, and because they are your friends.

Document 7: In Defense of Lincoln, May 20, 1864

Garrison was hardly Abraham Lincoln's biggest supporter. There was much about Lincoln and Lincoln's handling of the war that Garrison found objectionable. Yet when all was said and done, he felt he had to respect Lincoln's work, even in the face of opposition from Lincoln-haters among his friends. This excerpt eloquently explains Garrison's perspective on Lincoln.

Grant that there are many sad things to look in the face; grant that the whole of justice has not yet been done to the negro; grant that here and there grievances exist which are to be deplored and to be redressed; still, looking at the question broadly, comprehensively, and philosophically, I think the people will ask another question—whether they themselves have been one hair's breadth in advance of Abraham Lincoln? (Applause.) Whether they are not conscious that he has not only been fully up with him, but, on the whole, a little beyond them? (Applause.) As the stream cannot rise higher than the fountain, so the President of the United States, amenable to public sentiment, could not, if he wished to do it, far transcend public sentiment in any direction. (Applause.) For my own part, when I remember the trials through which he has passed, and the perils which have surrounded him—perils and trials unknown to any man, in any age of the world, in official station—when I remember how fearfully pro-slavery was the public sentiment of the North, to say nothing of the South—when I remember what he has had to deal with—when I remember how nearly a majority, even at this hour, is the seditious element of the North, and then remember that Abraham Lincoln has struck the chains from the limbs of more than three millions of slaves (applause); that he has expressed his earnest desire for the total abolition of slavery; that he has implored the Border States to get rid of it; that he has recognized the manhood and citizenship of the colored population of our country; that he has armed upwards of a hundred thousand of them, and recognized them as soldiers under the flag; when I remember that this Administration has recognized the independence of Liberia and Hayti; when I remember that it has struck a death blow at the foreign slave trade by granting the right of search; when I remember that we have now nearly reached the culmination of our great struggle for the suppression of the rebellion and its cause, I do not feel disposed, for one, to take this occasion, or any occasion, to say anything very harshly against Abraham Lincoln. (Loud and prolonged applause.)

Document 8: *Reelection, November 18, 1864*

Garrison had come to change his mind about the role of politics and violence in the antislavery struggle. This excerpt demonstrates the degree to which Garrison had come to realize that through these means alone would abolition ultimately come to pass.

The reelection of Mr. Lincoln, therefore, derives its significance and importance not only from its vast numerical power, but still more from the character and position of the mighty mass who gave him their suffrages. It is a decision from which there can be no appeal, except from the highest civilization to the lowest barbarism. It indicates incomparably greater attributes than can be found in mere physical supremacy—all of education, science, art, morality, religion in its best development, philanthropy in its highest aspirations, reform in its widest bearings. Hence, the government is stable beyond all precedent, notwithstanding the rebellious convulsions of the hour; and the administration of Mr. Lincoln has accorded to it a sanction and strength which no previous one—not excepting Washington's—has ever been able to secure.

The election has determined many things. First—it shows how great is the confidence of the people in the honesty, sagacity, administrative ability, and patriotic integrity of Abraham Lincoln. And yet, what efforts were left undone by some whose loyalty was unquestionable, and by all whose disloyalty was "palpable as a mountain," to utterly destroy that confidence, and cause his ignominious rejection? He was ridiculed and caricatured in every possible manner—represented (incoherently enough) as playing the part of tyrant and usurper, and yet being little better than an imbecile, having no mind of his own, but moulded by the abolition party, or by one or two members of his cabinet, "as clay in the hands of the potter"—as animated by a selfish desire to secure his re-election, no matter at what cost to the country—as disregarding all constitutional checks and limitations—as turning the war from its legitimate purpose to an unconstitutional end—as equally destitute of capacity and principle—as incurably afflicted with "nigger on the brain"—as oppressively bent on "subjugating" the rebellious South, and making conditions whereby union and peace were rendered impossible—as being too slow, and at the same time too fast—&c., &c. Moreover, it was said that he had lost the confidence of nearly all the prominent supporters of his administration, in Congress and out of it, who would in due time show their preference for another;—so that between such representations and the boastful predictions of his enemies, there seemed to be no chance for his success. As his most formidable loyal antagonist, General Fremont was early hurried into the field, with a flourish of trumpets and an assurance of easy victory which the result makes too ridiculous to need any comment.

Source Notes

Chapter 1: Slavery and Abolition

1. Quoted in William E. Cain, ed., *William Lloyd Garrison and the Fight Against Slavery: Selections from the* Liberator. Boston: Bedford Books of St. Martin's Press, 1995, p. 42.
2. Quoted in Russel B. Nye, *William Lloyd Garrison and the Humanitarian Reformers.* Boston: Little, Brown, 1955, p. 93.
3. Quoted in Nye, *William Lloyd Garrison and the Humanitarian Reformers*, p. 63.
4. Quoted in Henry Mayer, *All on Fire: William Lloyd Garrison and the Abolition of Slavery.* New York: St. Martin's Press, 1998, p. 242.
5. Quoted in Susanne Everett, *History of Slavery.* Edison, NJ: Chartwell Books, 1976, p. 102.
6. Quoted in William Dudley, ed., *Slavery.* San Diego: Greenhaven Press, 1992, p. 170.
7. Quoted in P.J. Staudenraus, *The African Colonization Movement 1816–1865.* New York: Columbia University Press, 1961, p. 203.
8. Quoted in Eric McKitrick, ed., *Slavery Defended: The Views of the Old South*, Englewood Cliffs, NJ: Prentice-Hall, 1963, p. 25.
9. Quoted in Staudenraus, *The African Colonization Movement*, p. 144.
10. Quoted in Dudley, *Slavery*, p. 165.
11. Quoted in Nye, *William Lloyd Garrison and the Humanitarian Reformers*, p. 47.
12. George Fitzhugh, *Sociology for the South, or the Failure of Free Society*, Richmond, VA: A. Morris, 1854, p. 246.
13. Quoted in Nye, *William Lloyd Garrison and the Humanitarian Reformers*, p. 47.
14. Quoted in William Summer Jenkins, *Pro-Slavery Thought in the Old South*. Chapel Hill: University of North Carolina Press, 1935, p. 231.
15. Quoted in Jenkins, *Pro-Slavery Thought in the Old South*, p. 250.
16. Quoted in Dudley, *Slavery*, p. 66.

Chapter 2: William Lloyd Garrison and the *Liberator*

17. Quoted in Nye, *William Lloyd Garrison and the Humanitarian Reformers*, p. 51.
18. Cain, *William Lloyd Garrison and the Fight Against Slavery*, p. 4.
19. Quoted in Mayer, *All on Fire*, p. 27.
20. Quoted in Mayer, *All on Fire*, p. 53.

21. Quoted in Mayer, *All on Fire*, pp. 49–50.

22. Quoted in Mayer, *All on Fire*, p. 38.

23. Quoted in Nye, *William Lloyd Garrison and the Humanitarian Reformers*, p. 21.

24. Quoted in Nye, *William Lloyd Garrison and the Humanitarian Reformers*, p. 22.

25. Quoted in Mayer, *All on Fire*, p. 66.

26. Quoted in Cain, *William Lloyd Garrison and the Fight Against Slavery*, p. 187.

27. Quoted in Mayer, *All on Fire*, p. 72.

28. Quoted in Mayer, *All on Fire*, p. 72.

29. Quoted in Dudley, *Slavery*, p. 191.

30. Quoted in Truman Nelson, ed., *Documents of Upheaval*. New York: Hill and Wang, 1966, p. 2.

31. Quoted in Nelson, *Documents of Upheaval*, p. xiii.

32. Quoted in Mayer, *All on Fire*, p. 105.

33. Quoted in Benjamin Quarles, *Black Abolitionists*. New York: Oxford University Press, 1969, p. 19.

34. Quoted in Mayer, *All on Fire*, p. 109.

35. Quoted in Nye, *William Lloyd Garrison and the Humanitarian Reformers*, p. 31.

36. Quoted in Mayer, *All on Fire*, p. 114.

37. Quoted in Mayer, *All on Fire*, p. 111.

38. Quoted in Dudley, *Slavery*, p. 174.

39. Quoted in Nye, *William Lloyd Garrison and the Humanitarian Reformers*, p. 50.

40. Quoted in Cain, *William Lloyd Garrison and the Fight Against Slavery*, p. 109.

41. Quoted in Margaret Stimmann Branson and Edward E. France, *The Human Side of Afro-American History*. Lexington, MA: Ginn, 1972, p. 76.

42. Quoted in Dudley, *Slavery*, p. 180.

43. Quoted in Nye, *William Lloyd Garrison and the Humanitarian Reformers*, p. 108.

44. Quoted in Cain, *William Lloyd Garrison and the Fight Against Slavery*, p. 103.

45. Quoted in Nelson, *Documents of Upheaval*, p. 6.

46. Quoted in Cain, *William Lloyd Garrison and the Fight Against Slavery*, p. 101.

47. Quoted in Cain, *William Lloyd Garrison and the Fight Against Slavery*, p. 30.

48. Quoted in Nelson, *Documents of Upheaval*, pp. 202–203.

49. Quoted in Nelson, *Documents of Upheaval*, p. 204.

50. Quoted in Mayer, *All on Fire*, p. 112.

51. Quoted in Dudley, *Slavery*, p. 173.

52. Quoted in Mayer, *All on Fire*, p. 124.

53. Quoted in Cain, *William Lloyd Garrison and the Fight Against Slavery*, p. 44.

54. Quoted in Dudley, *Slavery*, p. 159.

55. Quoted in Cain, *William Lloyd Garrison and the Fight Against Slavery*, p. 37.

56. Quoted in Nye, *William Lloyd Garrison and the Humanitarian Reformers*, p. 58.

57. Quoted in Mayer, *All on Fire*, p. 226.

58. Quoted in Cain, *William Lloyd Garrison and the Fight Against Slavery*, p. 36.

59. Quoted in Cain, *William Lloyd Garrison and the Fight Against Slavery*, p. 114.

60. Quoted in Mayer, *All on Fire*, p. 120.

61. Quoted in Nye, *William Lloyd Garrison and the Humanitarian Reformers*, p. 50.

62. Quoted in Nelson, *Documents of Upheaval*, p. 204.

Chapter 3: Philosophy

63. Quoted in Nye, *William Lloyd Garrison and the Humanitarian Reformers*, p. 109.

64. Quoted in Cain, *William Lloyd Garrison and the Fight Against Slavery*, p. 28.

65. Quoted in Mayer, *All on Fire*, p. 28.

66. Felicia Dorothea Hemans, *The Poetical Works of Felicia Dorothea Hemans*. London: Oxford University Press, 1914, p. 396.

67. Quoted in Mayer, *All on Fire*, p. 28.

68. Quoted in Mayer, *All on Fire*, p. 224.

69. Quoted in Nelson, *Documents of Upheaval*, p. 278.

70. Quoted in Nelson, *Documents of Upheaval*, p. 55.

71. Quoted in Mayer, *All on Fire*, p. 249.

72. Quoted in Jenkins, *Pro-Slavery Thought in the Old South*, p. 223.

73. Quoted in Nelson, *Documents of Upheaval*, p. 10.

74. Quoted in Nye, *William Lloyd Garrison and the Humanitarian Reformers*, p. 50.

75. Quoted in Cain, *William Lloyd Garrison and the Fight Against Slavery*, p. 104.

76. Quoted in Cain, *William Lloyd Garrison and the Fight Against Slavery*, p. 103.

77. Quoted in Cain, *William Lloyd Garrison and the Fight Against Slavery*, p. 156.
78. Quoted in Mayer, *All on Fire*, p. 237.
79. Quoted in Cain, *William Lloyd Garrison and the Fight Against Slavery*, p. 102.
80. Quoted in Cain, *William Lloyd Garrison and the Fight Against Slavery*, p. 104.
81. Quoted in Cain, *William Lloyd Garrison and the Fight Against Slavery*, p. 105.
82. Quoted in Nelson, *Documents of Upheaval*, p. 202.
83. Quoted in Cain, *William Lloyd Garrison and the Fight Against Slavery*, p. 38.
84. Quoted in Mayer, *All on Fire*, p. 121.
85. Quoted in Nye, *William Lloyd Garrison and the Humanitarian Reformers*, p. 20.
86. Quoted in Mayer, *All on Fire*, p. 176.
87. Quoted in Nelson, *Documents of Upheaval*, p. 56.
88. Quoted in Allan Nevins and Henry Steele Commager, *A Pocket History of the United States*. 6th ed. New York: Pocket Books, 1976, p. 85.
89. Quoted in Dudley, *Slavery*, p. 174.
90. Quoted in Branson and France, *The Human Side of Afro-American History*, p. 76.
91. Quoted in Nye, *William Lloyd Garrison and the Humanitarian Reformers*, p. 87.
92. Quoted in Nevins and Commager, *A Pocket History of the American People*, p. 85.
93. Quoted in Cain, *William Lloyd Garrison and the Fight Against Slavery*, p. 158.
94. Quoted in Nelson, *Documents of Upheaval*, p. 159.
95. Quoted in Mayer, *All on Fire*, p. 115.

Chapter 4: Reaction
96. Quoted in Nye, *William Lloyd Garrison and the Humanitarian Reformers*, p. 51.
97. Quoted in Everett, *History of Slavery*, 123.
98. Quoted in Nye, *William Lloyd Garrison and the Humanitarian Reformers*, p. 52.
99. Quoted in Nye, *William Lloyd Garrison and the Humanitarian Reformers*, p. 52.
100. Quoted in Nelson, *Documents of Upheaval*, p. 37.
101. Quoted in Dudley, *Slavery*, p. 159.

102. Quoted in Nye, *William Lloyd Garrison and the Humanitarian Reformers*, p. 54.

103. Quoted in Nelson, *Documents of Upheaval*, p. 39.

104. Quoted in Nye, *William Lloyd Garrison and the Humanitarian Reformers*, p. 98.

105. Quoted in Louis Filler, *The Crusade Against Slavery 1830–1860*. New York: Harper and Row, 1960, p. 58.

106. Quoted in Nye, *William Lloyd Garrison and the Humanitarian Reformers*, pp. 67–68.

107. Quoted in Mayer, *All on Fire*, p. 198.

108. Quoted in Nelson, *Documents of Upheaval*, p. 81.

109. Quoted in Nye, *William Lloyd Garrison and the Humanitarian Reformers*, p. 81.

110. Quoted in Nye, *William Lloyd Garrison and the Humanitarian Reformers*, p. 68.

111. Quoted in Nelson, *Documents of Upheaval*, p. 88.

112. Quoted in Branson and France, *The Human Side of Afro-American History*, p. 55.

113. Quoted in Nelson, *Documents of Upheaval*, p. 94.

114. Quoted in Mayer, *All on Fire*, p. 206.

115. Quoted in Cain, *William Lloyd Garrison and the Fight Against Slavery*, p. 40.

116. Quoted in Mayer, *All on Fire*, p. 124.

117. Quoted in Nye, *William Lloyd Garrison and the Humanitarian Reformers*, p. 118.

118. Quoted in Nye, *William Lloyd Garrison and the Humanitarian Reformers*, p. 68.

119. Quoted in Mayer, *All on Fire*, p. 118.

120. Quoted in Nelson, *Documents of Upheaval*, p. 161.

121. Quoted in Nye, *William Lloyd Garrison and the Humanitarian Reformers*, p. 110.

122. Quoted in Cain, *William Lloyd Garrison and the Fight Against Slavery*, p. 41.

123. Quoted in Mayer, *All on Fire*, p. 116.

124. Quoted in Filler, *The Crusade Against Slavery 1830–1860*, p. 59.

125. Quoted in Nye, *William Lloyd Garrison and the Humanitarian Reformers*, p. 75.

Chapter 5: Legacy

126. Quoted in Nevins and Commager, *A Pocket History of the American People*, p. 199.

127. Quoted in Mayer, *All on Fire*, p. 439.

128. Quoted in Nevins and Commager, *A Pocket History of the American People*, p. 206.

129. Quoted in Mayer, *All on Fire*, p. 444.

130. Quoted in Nye, *William Lloyd Garrison and the Humanitarian Reformers*, p. 158.

131. Quoted in Branson and France, *The Human Side of Afro-American History*, p. 79.

132. Quoted in Nye, *William Lloyd Garrison and the Humanitarian Reformers*, p. 167.

133. Quoted in Cain, *William Lloyd Garrison and the Fight Against Slavery*, p. 156.

134. Quoted in Nye, *William Lloyd Garrison and the Humanitarian Reformers*, p. 149.

135. Quoted in Mayer, *All on Fire*, p. 383.

136. Mayer, *All on Fire*, p. 487.

137. Quoted in Mayer, *All on Fire*, p. 489.

138. Quoted in Cain, *William Lloyd Garrison and the Fight Against Slavery*, pp. 171–72.

139. Quoted in Mayer, *All on Fire*, p. 598.

140. Quoted in Nelson, *Documents of Upheaval*, p. 281.

141. Quoted in James M. McPherson, *The Abolitionist Legacy*. Princeton, NJ: Princeton University Press, 1975, p. 90.

142. Quoted in McPherson, *The Abolitionist Legacy*, p. 89.

143. Quoted in Nye, *William Lloyd Garrison and the Humanitarian Reformers*, p. 194.

144. Mayer, *All on Fire*, p. 264.

145. Quoted in Nye, *William Lloyd Garrison and the Humanitarian Reformers*, p. 200.

146. Quoted in Mayer, *All on Fire*, p. 414.

For Further Reading

Stephen Currie, *Life of a Slave on a Southern Plantation*. San Diego: Lucent Books, 2000. Detailed descriptions of American slavery; useful context to Garrison's time and work.

——, *Slavery*. San Diego: Greenhaven Press, 1999. A careful examination of the attitudes and arguments surrounding slavery in the years preceding the Civil War, with particular emphasis on controversies such as colonization, immediate versus gradual emancipation, and slave revolts.

Frederick Douglass, *Escape from Slavery; The Boyhood of Frederick Douglass in His Own Words*. Ed. Michael McCurdy. New York: Knopf, 1994. Douglass was one of the great abolitionists and a longtime friend of Garrison's. Excerpts from his own life story.

Susanne Everett, *History of Slavery*. Edison, NJ: Chartwell Books, 1976. A consideration of slavery throughout history and around the world. Especially well illustrated. Includes material on Garrison, the *Liberator*, and other abolitionists.

William Loren Katz, *Breaking the Chains*. New York: Aladdin, 1998. An overview of slave revolts, with some information on their effect on slaveholders and abolitionists.

Mary Barr Sisson et al., *The Gathering Storm 1787–1829 : From the Framing of the Constitution to Walker's Appeal*. Broomall, PA: Chelsea House, 1996. Describes the context of slavery up to Garrison's founding of the *Liberator*. Includes information on slavery in the territories and abolition.

Richard Steins, *The Nation Divides: The Civil War (1820–1880)*. New York: Twenty-First Century Books, 1995. A description of the events leading up to the Civil War and afterwards, with emphasis on the breakup of the Union.

Joel Strangis, *Lewis Hayden and the War Against Slavery*. North Haven, CT: Linnet Books, 1999. Hayden was a runaway slave who became a member of Boston's black community. The book includes information on the *Liberator*.

The 19th Century and Abolition (Voices in African American History series). Columbus, OH: Modern Curriculum Press, 1994. A study of abolitionists and their times, including information about the *Liberator*.

Works Consulted

Stephen Bates, *If No News, Send Rumors.* New York: St. Martin's Press, 1989. Anecdotes relating to American journalism throughout history. Useful for establishing a sense of the journalistic standards of Garrison's day.

Margaret Stimmann Branson and Edward E. France, *The Human Side of Afro-American History.* Lexington, MA: Ginn, 1972. A sourcebook of readings on African American history. Includes excerpts from and about Garrison as well as discussion of slavery itself and other abolitionists.

William E. Cain, ed., *William Lloyd Garrison and the Fight Against Slavery: Selections from the* Liberator. Boston: Bedford Books of St. Martin's Press, 1995. A very useful and informative collection of various excerpts from the *Liberator,* covering immediatism, women's rights, pacifism, the Civil War, and much more. Includes clear and well-balanced commentary.

Lydia Maria Child, *An Appeal in Favor of That Class of Americans Called Africans.* 1836. Reprinted New York: Arno Press, 1968. A brief in favor of the rights of African Americans, in a tone very different from Garrison's. Child is moderate and conciliatory, but presents clear and forceful arguments throughout.

William Dudley, ed., *Slavery.* San Diego: Greenhaven Press, 1992. Documents relating to the history of slavery, with timelines and questions for discussion. Includes sections on abolition and the division of the nation.

Louis Filler, *The Crusade Against Slavery 1830–1860.* New York: Harper and Row, 1960. A good overview of abolitionism; Filler sees Garrison as perhaps the most influential of all abolitionists, but he puts the *Liberator* firmly in context as well.

George Fitzhugh, *Sociology for the South, or the Failure of Free Society*, Richmond, VA: A. Morris, 1854. The most notorious, perhaps, of all Southern apologists for slavery. An excellent example of the "positive good" argument.

Felicia Dorothea Hemans, *The Poetical Works of Felicia Dorothea Hemans.* London: Oxford University Press, 1914. The poems of one of Garrison's favorite authors.

William Sumner Jenkins, *Pro-Slavery Thought in the Old South*. Chapel Hill: University of North Carolina Press, 1935. Defenses of slavery advanced by Southerners, including many direct quotations.

Henry Mayer, *All on Fire: William Lloyd Garrison and the Abolition of Slavery*. New York: St. Martin's Press, 1998. The essential book on the life and work of Garrison; more than six hundred pages of well-written and insightful analysis. Thorough and thought-provoking.

Eric McKitrick, ed., *Slavery Defended: The Views of the Old South*. Englewood Cliffs, NJ: Prentice-Hall, 1963. Slavery from the Southern perspective; a collection of primary sources.

James M. McPherson, *The Abolitionist Legacy*. Princeton, NJ: Princeton University Press, 1975. Useful for Garrison's role in Reconstruction; draws interesting connections between the abolitionists and later African American history.

Herbert Mitgang, ed., *Lincoln As They Saw Him*. New York: Rinehart and Company, 1956. A long and interesting book quoting excerpts from newspapers regarding Abraham Lincoln. Though the *Liberator* is not quoted directly, the book is helpful for understanding newspapers of the time and public reaction toward anti-slavery thought.

Truman Nelson, ed., *Documents of Upheaval*. New York: Hill and Wang, 1966. Another collection of excerpts from the *Liberator*, including somewhat different selections from Cain's (see entry above). The commentary is noticeably uncritical of Garrison.

Allan Nevins and Henry Steele Commager, *A Pocket History of the United States*. 6th ed. New York: Pocket Books, 1976. A one-volume overview of U.S. history. Clear though brief presentations of events and people.

Russel B. Nye, *William Lloyd Garrison and the Humanitarian Reformers*. Boston: Little, Brown, 1955. A carefully written, relatively short biography focusing on Garrison's career and his place within the abolition movement.

David Powell, *Tom Paine: The Greatest Exile*. New York: St. Martin's Press, 1985. Interesting profile of Thomas Paine; he and Garrison had many similarities in temperament and style.

Benjamin Quarles, *Black Abolitionists*. New York: Oxford University Press, 1969. A study of African Americans who fought slavery. Assesses Garrison as a strong supporter of blacks' rights and a strong influence on those who fought to free the slaves.

Louis Ruchames, *The Abolitionists: A Collection of Their Writings*. New York: G.P. Putnam's Sons, 1963. Primary source documents, including some of Garrison's.

P.J. Staudenraus, *The African Colonization Movement 1816–1865*. New York: Columbia University Press, 1961. A thorough account of the colonization movement: its supporters, its opponents, and the controversies it sparked.

Jessamyn West, ed., *The Quaker Reader*. New York: Viking, 1962. Documents on Quakers and Quakerism, including abolitionist sentiment.

Index

Picture Credits

About the Author

Stephen Currie is the author of more than forty books, including a number of works on history and some historical fiction. Among his books for Lucent are *Life in a Wild West Show*, *The Olympic Games*, and *Adoption*. He is also a teacher. He grew up in Illinois and now lives with his family in upstate New York.